The Ever Rolling Stream

by

Bill Tandy

Acknowledgement

To Anne
and all nurses everywhere

All the corpses in the world are chemically identical,
but living individuals are not.

Carl Gustav Jung

FOREWORD

Time like an ever rolling stream
Bears all its sons away.

H.F. Lyte

Following the publication of a book about the Foresters I knew in the days before the National Health Service, when I became a doctor in the Forest of Dean after spending some years in India, numerous people have asked me to write a book about other folk I have met. So here it is: not an autobiography, just a mixed bag of memories. Memories of individual people whom time, like an ever rolling stream, has now borne away.

Published by
Douglas Mclean

at

THE FOREST BOOK SHOP
32 Market Place, Coleford, Glos. GL16 8AA

Printed by LOGOS
Cinderford, Glos. GL14 2PQ

ISBN 0 946 252 14 9

Contents

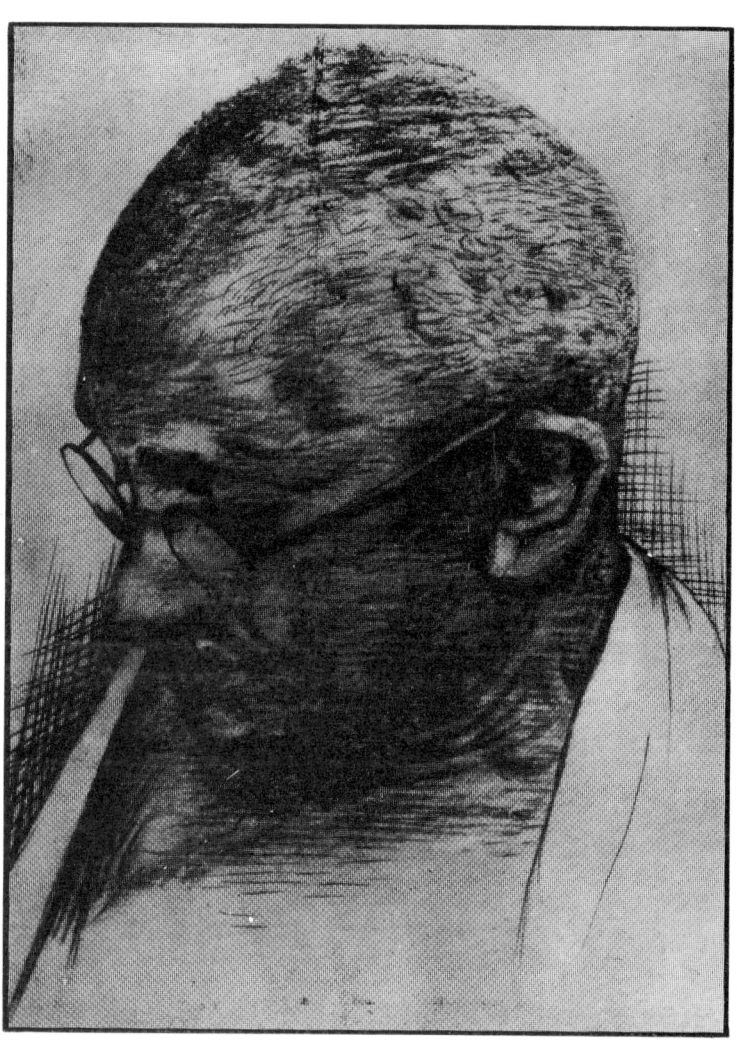

Chapter One
Chief

We wolf-cubs called him "Chief"; not "the Chief", and never Mr. Chamberlain.

I enjoyed being a wolf-cub many years ago. The cubs were different from the boys I had to mix with at the dreadful fee-paying Preparatory School my parents sent me to. I hero-worshipped Chief as did all the other cubs, he had that sort of charisma. He had no need to be strict, we obeyed him instantly and gave him all our loyalty. He was in his early twenties, tall, with the lean build of an athlete, a fresh face, and fair untidy hair. He was a lover of the open air and the countryside, although his job was in an office in Birmingham, accountancy I think it was.

About a mile from where I lived there was a large wood, it is a housing estate now. Chief had got permission to use it for scouting. He taught us all the tenderfoot lore, both in the wood and in the classroom where we met during the winter months. Sometimes we spent a weekend camping in the wood, then at dusk, we sat around the camp fire with mugs of hot cocoa and sang songs, or listened to the stories Chief told us, and when there was a full moon he made us sit in silence and watch it rise. He made that wood an enchanted place for me. It opened up a new world; a world of small wild animals that left their footmarks on the ground, of birds and trees and wild flowers. At home I used to lie in bed before I went to sleep visualising that wood and all the living things of wonder that lived in it. It seemed a sort of wild Garden of Eden compared with the tidy suburban garden of my home.

I had a pretty stable home life, we were a united family. My father was a kind, gentle, generous man whose life consisted of his home, his business, his church and his garden; with these he seemed content. My mother, with the aid of resident domestics kept the home going with a daily routine which was punctual and calm.

I was born with a fairly severe degree of astigmatism which meant that from a very early age I had to wear spectacles, and I loathed them, they made me self-conscious, and feel different from other boys. I had to be careful about playing rough games. Chief knew how I detested those spectacles, he knew about that awful school where I was being bullied and nicknamed "Four Eyes"; I never talked to him about it, but somehow he made me feel he knew. It was sort of comforting, like having a much older caring brother.

The family was on their annual summer sea-side holiday at Rhos-on-Sea in North Wales during the August of 1914 when war broke out. I was nine years old, nearly ten and did not really understand what it meant. It was an

1

opportunity to play a new game with my cousin - hunting German spies. I was not involved in the upheaval, it was only on the return from the holiday at the end of the month that I realised that it was serious. I went to Cubs as usual, Chief was there in Khaki uniform, wearing a Sam Browne and with a Subaltern's pip on each shoulder. He had come to say goodbye; he had enlisted at the outbreak of war. He told us he would soon be going to France, but would not be away for long; he would soon be back, it wouldn't take long to teach those Germans a lesson for what they had done to little Belgium.

Cubs' nights were much duller after he left. His brother took over the pack to keep it together until Chief returned. He was an older man; from what I remember of him he had not much understanding of small boys, he was more interested in books than the countryside. He never took us to the wood, but we cubs loyally stuck together waiting for Chief's return after he had taught the Germans their lesson.

Nearly three months later I was a few minutes late arriving at Cubs. When I opened the door and went inside, instead of the usual hub-bub it was all quiet; the other cubs were talking together in hushed voices and looking very solemn. One of them came up to me and whispered "There's been a telegram. Chief has been killed in France". I suddenly went numb; I felt I was going to choke. I did not want to stay and talk about it with the other boys, so I slipped away home.

As I climbed the stairs to my bedroom, my mother called out "You're back very soon". "Chief has been killed in France", I replied chokingly. I went into my room, lay on the bed and sobbed. My mother came up to try to comfort me, but I did not want to be comforted, all I wanted was Chief not to be dead, but he was, and the finality of it was more than I could bear. I wanted to be left alone with my misery. That morning my life had not extended beyond home, school and cubs. Now, suddenly, there was also a large, dreadful, threatening, cruel world that had taken Chief away from me.

Grief can be a devastating experience for a child. I felt no-one, not even my parents, understood; I could not talk about it. I suppose my parents' attitude was "Poor lad, he's very upset. He will get over it. How sad about that nice Mr. Chamberlain".

Mixed with my grief was hatred and anger. I hated the Germans. I hated the Kaiser. They had killed Chief. I hated the war. Gradually the hatred and anger gave way to rebelliousness. About a year after Chief's death I left the Preparatory School and went to King Edward's. I was not bullied there, it was a relief not to be "Four Eyes" anymore. But I took that rebelliousness with me, I became a rebel, it often got me into trouble. I don't think it has ever left me!

Chief is but a hazy memory now after all the many years; like a mist in the past which has almost disappeared. I expect he was really a pretty ordinary young man, but to a Wolf Cub he was a marvellous person. I owe my love of the wild things of nature to him; and also a permanent rebelliousness against, and mistrust of, authority, born of my childhood grief at his slaughter.

2

Chapter Two

The Nameless One

There were no A-level examinations in schools in 1922, entrance to a University was by an examination called Matriculation. After passing that the first year medical student entered Medical School and studied Physics, Chemistry and Biology, the last being Zoology and Botany combined. Nowadays these subjects are taken at A-level at school. The first year at Medical School in the twenties seemed to the student to be far removed from doctoring, the examination at the end of it was regarded as just a nuisance of a hurdle to be got over before we could start the real thing. The start of the second year seemed a long way away, and the third year, when we would enter the hospital wards, aeons away. We just crammed the Physics and the inorganic chemistry. We dissected the disgusting dog-fish which had been preserved in formalin. We regarded Botany as a bore, what had monocotyledons and dicotyledons to do with doctoring? Necessary perhaps in the apothecary days of more than a century ago, but not now.

Being a second-year student was different, the subjects now were human physiology and anatomy, we were getting nearer doctoring. True we had to play about with giving electrical stimuli to the muscles of a frog's leg in the practical physiology laboratory to show us what a reflex action was. But now we each had our own human skeleton to study, and there was the dissecting room where we dissected a human body, a welcome change from the malodorous formalin-soaked dog-fish.

We were a bit apprehensive before we entered the dissecting room for the first time - a sort of curiosity mixed with awe. We could not imagine what it would be like; I, like most of the other students, had never seen a dead body. A Scot, Professor James Brash, was in charge of the anatomy department. He was not only a good teacher, he was strict, he insisted that the dead bodies, called subjects, be treated with reverence. Smoking in the dissecting room was banned, and laughter or any suggestion of hilarity was frowned upon. When we first went into the dissecting room we saw a long row of trestle tables on each of which was a corpse which had been injected with a preservative, and also a red dye to show up the blood vessels. Two students were assigned to a body; each dissected a limb himself, but they shared the abdomen, thorax and difficult head and neck.

There was a sort of secrecy about where the bodies had been obtained from, I don't know why, perhaps a bit of guilt still hanging about from the old body-snatching, grave-robbing days. A few of the subjects had been bequeathed in the wills of their owners "to benefit medical science". Most of them came from the Workhouse Infirmaries, poor old men and women who had died with no relatives or friends to claim them and give them a decent burial - the lonely and the destitute ones of the world, tramps and loners and alcoholics, the cast-offs of society. They had ended up in the dissecting room of a medical school, nameless.

The subject my friend and I shared was an emaciated old man, obviously obtained from a Workhouse Infirmary. We were shown how to reflect the skin and expose the under-lying muscles, learning their names and where and how they were attached to the bones. Nerves and blood vessels were meticulously dissected and the branches traced from their origins to their terminations, their names being memorised...We very soon lost any squeamishness as we concentrated on the dissection and forgot that it was a man's body we were cutting apart.

That nameless old man lying there on the trestle table, his skin flayed, and his muscles and organs laid bare, had once been a baby. A microscopic fertilised egg-cell, activated by some transcendental force, had fissioned and re-fissioned and had been nestled in a woman's body for forty creative weeks to become a person: that was a marvel, and it was a mystery. I wonder what his life history was. What chance in life had that baby had? What was he like when those blood-vessels were filled with circulating oxygenated blood, when the nerves were transmitting small electrical currents, and the muscles of his face showed his emotions? He was one of life's failures I suppose. He probably never had much of a fair chance from the word go. I can imagine him in torn and dirty clothes, smelly and unshaven, with matted hair, perhaps pushing an old pram containing all his worldly possessions, with no permanent resting place; finally being admitted to the Workhouse Infirmary and dying there, and then ending up a nameless subject on the trestle-table of the Medical School's anatomy dissecting room, useless to Society until then. Maybe in his wanderings, sleeping rough in the countryside, he had been more in harmony with nature, with the secret heart of the beauty and mystery of the act of creation, than the successful business people on their interior-sprung mattresses in their pretentious suburban houses. Maybe.

I am grateful to that old man. The knowledge of anatomy I subsequently acquired was founded on my dissection of his dead nameless body. My gratitude is mingled with a kind of pity. I can understand why Professor Brash insisted that the anatomy subjects should always be treated with reverence by light-hearted irreverent youth.

Chapter Three

The Big Black Beetle

When you walked behind him he looked just like an enormous black beetle. Dressed in a black morning coat with tails, tall and burly with broad
shoulders and a slight stoop, he shambled rumbustiously along the hospital
corridors from ward to ward, his house surgeon at his side, and a collection
of students bringing up the rear. He appeared to tower like a giant over
everybody.

His name was Leonard Gamgee, honorary Professor of Surgery at the
Birmingham General Hospital. He was an extrovert, an exhibitionist, a
dogmatist, and a natural born teacher.

On the first day we attended hospital as third year students he took us on
a ward round. The hospital world was a new experience for us, something
we had been looking forward to for a long time. We felt like intruders in a
place where everyone else seemed so much at home, who knew what they
were doing and where they were going. We did not know our way about in
this world of women in uniforms, men in white coats, and patients in rows
of beds.

This first ward round he called his "Sherlock Holmes" lecture. We students clustered around a patient's bed, Gamgee and his house suregon at
the head with the Ward Sister and a nurse standing opposite to him on the
other side. The patients never seemed to mind being talked about, they
liked looking at the young faces around them, a welcome break to the
monotonous hospital routine. When their tummies were being examined
by a succession of palpitating hands, they felt important, somebody special; everyone likes to feel important, some of them had never been important before.

The entourage stopped at the first bed. "You are now starting your clinical life", announced the Professor, "you have got to learn to use your powers of observation, to be like Sherlock Holmes. Laboratory tests and X-ray
photographs have their place, but a secondary place. It is what you observe
for yourselves that is most important. You have been given five senses by
your Creator, you must learn to use and develop them". We listened to this
imposing man with a feeling of awe and reverence at his wisdom, we
regarded him as a sort of oracle, prepared to believe his every word as eter-
nal truth.

"First, your sense of sight", said the Oracle, "look at the patient. Is he fat
or thin and wasted? What is the colour of his skin, is he pale? Look at the
expression on his face and at his eyes. Look at his hands, look at the
patient". We all looked.

5

"Now your sense of hearing: listen to the patient. Listen to what he says and how he says it. Listen to his breathing. Listen to any gurgling sounds in his abdomen". He paused. We all listened. We couldn't hear anything.

"Your sense of touch: a most important sense. You can touch any part of his exterior and feel inside an orifice. Always touch lightly, gently and sensitively. This man has a large liver, you can feel the edge of it going up and down as he breathes. Feel it, each of you". We put our clumsy fingers on the man's abdomen and pretended we could feel the liver's edge.

"Your sense of smell: smell his breath, smell any discharge. Smell his urine". He picked up a specimen glass of urine that had been placed on the patient's locker. He held it to his nose and sniffed, then passed it round for us all to have a smell. We each dutifully smelt it.

"Your fifth sense, the sense of taste. I suppose you think you won't need that. But what did the old physicians in bygone days do to diagnose diabetes? They tasted it to see if it tasted sweet. Suppose one day you urgently need to know if a patient has sugar and you have no chemical tests at hand. What will you do? You will taste it. This patient has diabetes". He picked up the speciment glass of urine again, dipped a finger in it, and touched his tongue. Then he passed the glass round for each of us to use his sense of taste. When the last student had obeyed and handed back the glass he gave us all a withering and pitying look. "Gentlemen," he said (he always ignored the women students; he had opposed their admission to the medical school; he believed that the Almighty had created women to be nurses and men to be doctors). "Gentlemen, I have been wasting my time. I have been trying to teach you to use your powers of observation, to be like Sherlock Holmes. Did you not observe that whereas I put my middle finger in the urine, I put my ring finger in my mouth?" We felt like a bunch of fools, we had all fallen for it. We dared not look at the expressions on the faces of the Ward Sister and her nurse. Oh! he had taught us something alright.

Gamgee was quite a Sherlock Holmes himself. His own powers of observation were phenomenal, almost uncanny, and he had a great sense of humour. At his Out-patient sessions he would sit at the desk with a bunch of adulating students standing behind him. He would look at each patient and without asking any questions of him or doing any examination would turn round and tell the students what the man's occupation was and the probable diagnosis. In nine times out of ten he would be right.

I remember one young man coming to his Out-patient session suffering from acute orchitis due to gonorrhoea. The patient lay on the couch while Gamgee examined him. "And how do you think you got that?", Gamgee sternly asked him. The young man put on an innocent air, "'I don't know doctor", he replied, "I think I must have strained myself, lifting at work, or turning over in bed, or something". Gamgee grunted, then turned round and walked over to the wash-hand basin to wash his hands. As he did so he beckoned the students over. "The first symptom of gonorrhoea is lying", he told them, "but that young fellow got very near the truth when he said he did it turning over in bed".

Gamgee was in great demand as a medical expert in the Law Courts. In the witness box he was a most imposing figure, like some great actor; he made a big impression on the Jury. One Barrister,tried to refute Gamgee's opinion by producing a text book of surgery and quoting from it. The Professor drew himself up to his full height, glowered at the Barrister, and said, "Textbooks are not evidence. I am my own textbook of surgery".

On another occasion he was giving expert evidence on behalf of an Insurance company in a compensation case. He was convinced the litigant was malingering. The man limped badly as with apparent difficulty he made his way across the Court to the Witness Box. The man won his case, much to the anger of Gamgee. As he left the Court he saw the man walk down the road quite briskly and normally. The infuriated Gamgee rushed up to him, caught him by the nape of his neck and the seat of the trousers and frog-marched him back to the Court where he protested to the Judge that there had been a miscarriage of justice. The Judge was trying another case, and only the threat of being committed for contempt of Court induced the enraged Professor to let go his grip.

Gamgee had a long standing fued with Lord Moynihan of Leeds over the surgical treatment of gastric ulcer. Moynihan was a truly great surgeon, and, like Gamgee, an exhibitionist. He has presented Leeds Museum with plaster casts of his hands, I believe. I think Gamgee was really jealous that another provincial surgeon should have such a wide reputation. At one surgical convention he met Moynihan and remonstrated with him because he had recently operated on his own wife when she had an attack of acute appendicitis. In Gamgee's opinion it was a most unethical thing to do, and he told him so to his face. "And why is my wife not entitled to the finest surgeon she can get?" Moynihand asked. For once Gamgee was at a loss for a reply.

Leonard Gamgee was not a particularly great operating surgeon, but he was a great character and a magnificent teacher and lively reconteur. He had a funny story to emphasise every important point in surgery. While operating he never stopped talking, telling humorous anecdotes, and instructing his dressers in the principles of the art of surgery. He lived until well into his nineties. Perhaps it is that I am growing old, but I have a feeling that they don't make any Leonard Gamgees anymore.

Chapter Four

The Queens

If you had been in Birmingham in the late 1920's and had walked down Bath Row from Five Ways you would have noticed a large Victorian Building about three hundred yards down on the left hand side. It was a drab looking building in dreary surroundings, with noisy trams passing up and down the road outside. It was the Queen's Hospital, one of the two teaching hospitals attached to the Birmingham University Medical School. It is no longer the Queens, in its place is the Birmingham Accident Hospital. The teaching hospital for Birmingham is now the Queen Elizabeth Hospital, which in the 1920's was just the dream of a few forward looking people, and had not even reached the drawing board. It was at the Queen's at that time, in the later half of the 1920's, that I spent some time as a newly fledged medico doing three resident house appointments.

Every hospital has its own individual atmosphere which is dependent not just on bricks and mortar and concrete, but on the attitude of the people who work in it. There was something about the atmosphere in the Queen's which was warm and friendly, felt by patients and staff alike. It was a Voluntary Hospital, state bureaucracy could not in those days impose its cold and clammy hand. The resident medical staff were only temporarily a part of it, but they absorbed the atmosphere, enjoyed and appreciated it, and added to it a certain degree of gaiety and humour because of their youth. Until recently they had been carefree undergraduates. In later years we look back on our Queen's days with much affection, and recall the personalities and individualists amongst the Honorary Medical Staff, the Nursing Staff, and the more humble domestics and porters. Working there had helped to mould us into practising doctors; we had learnt to accept responsibilities, to make quick decisions, and to beware of the pitfalls that can trap the unwary.

We received a pound a week as salary, none of us were married, who could marry on £50 a year? Our living quarters were pretty primitive, and the food was atrocious. By and large we put up with it all without grumbling, despite the long hours on duty and the disturbed sleep. After all, our chiefs were giving their services to the hospital for nothing, and we felt we were lucky to get the job of being their housemen, we were "getting experience". Except for the few that were big-headed, we discovered that we could also learn a lot from an experienced Ward Sister. Some of them had been Sisters on the same ward for years, their whole life consisting of running their ward and gossiping in the Sisters' sitting room in the Nurses' Home when off duty.

They appeared to have no life at all outside the hospital.

One Sister had been in charge of the same surgical ward for about thirty years, and had known my Chief when he had been a student dresser. She ran her ward highly efficiently and with strict rules, it was *her* ward. One rule was that every patient in the ward had to be given three grains of calomel every Friday night. It had been a rule for thirty years, it was her order, and must be obeyed. But if my Chief tried to remonstrate with her about it she would stiffen up, fix him with a steely eye, and say: "I take three grains of calomel myself every Friday night. It has never done *me* any harm." And my Chief would wilt before her militant stance. "Who is this one-time dresser who dares to challenge my authority?" she seemed to be implying. He was the Professor of Surgery at the Queen's Hospital, but he retreated. She could be a real tyrant, especially to the student nurses and the medical students, yet when she did anything for a patient it was remarkable what gentle hands this severe and formidable woman had. Her experienced eye could detect immediately the slightest change for the worse or for the better in a patient on her ward.

In the grounds at the back of the hospital was the Nurses' Home, known of course, as in most teaching hospitals, as Virginity Palace. No male had ever entered it, we housemen hardly dare even look at it. I can remember the bird-cage containing the Matron's parrot that on most fine days stood outside the front door. The only other pet was a cat belonging to the Assistant Matron, Miss Pomphrey. She was an elderly woman, plump, white-haired and dignified, who showed nothing but scorn and contempt towards all students and housemen. She was greatly attached to her cat, which was an enormous, ugly, emasculated creature, quite revolting to look at. During the time I was at the Queen's it developed an unpleasant habit of going into one of the wards and settling down to sleep under a patients' bed. After a while we noticed, and so did some of the nurses, that when this happened the patient died soon afterwards. It was quite uncanny.

One day as we were having our evening meal a house surgeon came in, and as he sat down he said: "I've just seen old Pomphrey's cat under the bed of a hernia case. It can't do much harm there." Some time later during the meal the telephone rang to say this house surgeon was wanted urgently on one of the wards. He hurried off and returned later looking as though he had had some sort of a shock. In a husky voice he said: "You remember that hernia case I told you about that had Pomphrey's cat under his bed? Well, he's just suddenly died from a pulmonary embolism."

We all decided there and then that enough was enough and that something must be done about the Assistant Matron's cat. Later the same night a couple of housemen managed to catch the cat; it was chloroformed, put into a sack together with a brick and flung into the canal which was at the back of the hospital. The next day Miss Pomphrey was in a state of much agitation looking for her cat, so she elicited the help of Lacey, the mortuary porter.

Lacey was a great character who had been employed at the hospital many years, about as many as Miss Pomphrey. They were both very much of the permanent establishment. His domain was the mortuary, where he reigned supreme, presiding over all the autopsies in a truly regal manner. He had great respect for the Matron and the Assistant Matron. He knew all the hospital gossip, and had known many generations of housemen and knew their ways.

It didn't take him very long to fish that cat out of the canal. He then went to Miss Pomphrey and said: "I have some sad news for you. Your cat had fallen into the canal and is drowned. But I have got it out, and I've arranged for it to have a real Christian burial. I have sewn it up inside one of Professor Emanuel's patients". Some months later I became Professor Emanuel's house physician, and one day I related this story to him. He listened with a grave face and then said: "If that body should be dug up many centuries hence it will revolutionise science."

One day I had just left the lodge at the entrance hall of the hospital where I had been answering the telephone when I met the Midwifery District Sister. She was a woman in her fifties, very experienced at her job, and for whom I had great regard. She was in uniform, had her black bag with her, and was on the way out. I gave her a greeting: "Hello Sister, off to a case I see". "I'm just off to see what a couple of Egyptian students are doing," she replied, "they have been gone quite a while".

We had quite a lot of students from Egypt about that time, these two were doing their month of practical obstetrics. All the students had to spend a month, in pairs, living in the hospital on call for confinements in the District. It was obligatory for them to attend at least twenty cases, and they were under the control of the District Sister. The custom was for her to accompany them on their first four cases to learn the ropes and after that they were on their own. Many students, now doctors, had been through her hands and learnt from her the basic rudiments of domiciliary midwifery. The district round the hospital was very poor and slummy, and they learnt what to do about fleas and bugs. After they had done their twenty cases they would do no more midwifery, except reading about it for their final examination, until they had qualified and went into general practice, when they would be called in by district midwives who needed help with a difficult delivery.

The emphasis in training doctors in those days was not on ante-natal care as it is now. As there was also no Flying Squad or National Blood Transfusion Service it is not surprising that the maternal and natal mortalities were what they were fifty years ago.

However, I met the District Sister again some time later as she was returning from her visit. "Hello Sister," I said, "how were your Gypos getting along?" Her shoulders started to shake and I could see that she couldn't control her face, then she burst out laughing. "What's the great joke, Sister?" I asked her. "Well", she replied, "when I got there the woman had been delivered and seemed quite well and happy. One of the Egyptians was sitting on the floor washing the baby in a basin, and the other one was standing on the top of a step-ladder washing the ceiling. 'Whatever are you doing up there?' I asked him, and he looked down on me and said: 'Seestur, et ees ze enema, ze enema'" Higginson's enema syringes were used in those days routinely.

One morning each week was T's and A's day, a sort of mini-nightmare. The shambles began when about twenty children with their mothers were assembled by the Casualty Sister in a corner of the large Out-patient Hall. One by one, each child would be taken from its mother into the Casualty Operating Theatre. There it would be anaesthetised with open ether by a houseman, and the E.N.T. Surgeon would enucleate the tonsils and scrape away the adenoids. The child would then be turned on its side, wrapped in a blanket, and carried to a recovery room where it would be reunited with its mother. Later, after the child had recovered consciousness it would be visited by the houseman and have its throat inspected, the bewildered child struggling and clenching its jaws in protest. If there was no bleeding from the tonsil beds it was sent home with its mother, usually travelling on a tram. Many a distressed, anxious woman would be embarrassed when her child vomited stale blood clots on the floor of the tram and had to face an indignant bus conductor. I wonder how many children underwent this ordeal quite unnecessarily according to today's attitude to enlarged tonsils.

When the E.N.T. Surgeon had finished his list of tonsillectomies and the nurses had cleaned up all the blood and mess in the theatre it would be the turn of the Casualty House Surgeon to start his list of circumcisions, which were even more unnecessary than the tonsillectomies; both operations had a mortality and morbidity rate. The number of these operations performed today are mercifully very much less.

One day, I remember, when there had been a bit of a mix-up with one of the tonsil children, an indignant woman was seen holding aloft her naked son, who still had his enlarged tonsils and also had a strip of surgical gauze soaked in friar's balsam where his foreskin should have been, demanding of a tired and harassed Casualty Sister: "What have they been and gone and done to my poor little Alfie?"

Each general house surgeon had a weekly ritual known as his "bougie brigade". One afternoon, my day was Tuesday, a dozen or so elderly gentlemen, some of them looking rather decrepit, would assemble in a far corner of the waiting hall. They were all suffering from a stricture of the urethra, the relic of an attack of gonorrhoea many years previously. They knew that if the stricture was not dilated at regular intervals it would gradually contract and they would be in trouble; as it would be impossible for them to empty their bladders.

The passage was kept open by the insertion at intervals of bougies. These were steel rods of graduated sizes and were passed into the bladder beyond the stricture gradually dilating it as each bougie of increasing diameter was passed. No local anaesthetic was available in those days. The relief was only temporary for a month or two as the stricture would gradually contract again necessitating another dilation with the bougies.

Every six months there would be a change of house surgeon and the poor old men would wait trembling with anxiety wondering how gentle or how rough the new young doctor would be. By the time I had become a house surgeon they had devised a splendid scheme. As each old gentleman walked in he paused before getting himself onto the couch, and put a packet of ten Gold Flake cigarettes on the table next to the tray that contained the bougies, lying there all shining and sterile and fearsome.

If the young house surgeon passed the bougies painlessly the packet was left on the table, but if the victim had suffered any pain while the bougie was being passed, then as he got off the couch when the ordeal was over and buttoned up his trousers the old man would slip the Gold Flake packet into the pocket of his jacket.

To have a week's supply of cigarettes free when one only earned a pound a week was quite a consideration. It was a marvellous penance for the misdeeds of their youth for these old men to teach young doctors to be gentle with their hands, more constructive than any number of Hail Mary's. Whichever of them it was who first hit on the idea of the "Gold Flake racket" did a lasting service to the training of scores of doctors.

My surgical chief, Professor Billington, was a quiet relaxed man, who refused to hurry or be hurried. When in the theatre he never displayed those melodramatic outbursts of angry exhibitionism so much beloved by some of the surgeons of those times. While he was operating all was as still and quiet as a Quaker Meeting. He was a slow operator, taking a long time over his operations. I had to assist him and I soon discovered why he had the reputation of being so slow, it was because he was so gentle, so meticulous, handling human tissue with the utmost delicacy, as if with reverence. I never had any trouble with post-operative shock with his cases. This was many years before the introduction of intravenous anaesthesia and the muscle relaxants that are in use today, then it was chloroform, ether, and nitrous oxide gas.

His knowledge of anatomy was superlative, the competent way his fingers worked with human tissue made me feel profoundly ignorant. The ordinary hospital patient in those days regarded a surgeon as someone cold and ruthless, almost a butcher, they dreaded falling into the hands of one, when they would feel like lambs being led to the slaughter. Yet somehow my chief with his quiet demeanour seemed able to dispel all their fear.

He had one particular strange belief. He believed that what we now call a neurosis in a middle-aged woman was caused by the fact that she suffered from dropped kidneys. He was of the opinion that the drag and nag of a dropped or mobile kidney was the cause of her neurotic symptoms. And he believed that he could cure them by fixing their kidneys so that they could no longer move.

He had devised an operation for this by which he stitched the kidney securely to the bottom rib. He quite sincerely, almost obsessively, believed his theory, and wrote a book on the subject describing his operation. He was rather derided by some of his surgical colleagues because of his unorthodox views concerning dropped kidneys. One issue of the students' magazines published the following irreverent song, to the tune of "I'm forever blowing bubbles". It ran as follows:

I'm forever fixing kidneys,
Floating kidneys on the rib;

They drop so low,
Nearly reach the toe,
Then by my op. all symptoms go.
Someone's always smiling,
But I'm an awful nib
When I'm deftly fixing kidneys,
Floating kidneys on the rib.

But my chief was quite unmoved by all criticism, and certainly there were any number of doctors who referred cases to him for operation, so he must have had some satisfactory results. The cult of Freudian psycho-analysis had just appeared on the scene, whether a follow up of cases would prove that his operation was any more or any less effective than the analyst's couch in the treatment of neurosis would be interesting to find out.

When he had finished his operating session he always spent half-an-hour relaxing over a pot of tea in the surgeon's changing room, his H.S. being expected to stay with him. He would often then be in a chatty, almost expansive mood, discussing cases and reminiscing. He would often talk of the days when he had been Assistant Surgeon to Jordan Lloyd, a legendary figure at the Queen's who had been a famous surgeon and eccentric. He also told me about another surgeon of the past, Morrison, (nicknamed The Prophet) a contemporary of Jordan Lloyd, who was very religious and very fussy.

Before every operation, Morrison having donned his mask and sterile gown and gloves, would retire to a corner of the theatre, fold his hands together, and say a little prayer. One day he had a particularly complicated case to deal with and so he asked Jordan Lloyd to help him. As he was retiring to his corner to say his little prayer, Jordon Lloyd called over to him, "Morrison! I consider this case to be so serious that we should not call in any unprofessional aid".

Another day, while Morrison was operating, Jordan Lloyd went into the theatre to say something to him, but without first donning a gown and mask. "Go away, Lloyd, go away", said Morrison, "You'll infect my case". To which Jordan Lloyd replied, "Morrison, when my breath becomes so foul that it can infect a case of haemorrhoids I'll give up surgery".

I had passed the stage of feeling the full flush of glory at having my name on the Medical Register. Now, working with my chief, I felt rather humbled and abysmally ignorant, alongside his skill and knowledge and experience. I started pondering whether to start reading for the primary F.R.C.S. examination. At one of the post operative tea sessions I hesitatingly mentioned this to my chief. "Generalise before you specialise", he said. He told me that I should get a house physician's appointment and learn what the physicians can do. "Put in for Professor Emanuel's houseship", he said.

Having been so advised I thought it only right to take his advice, and duly applied for the appointment. Professor Emanual went by the nickname of Wiggy. Why, I never found out, but everybody called him Wiggy, never of course to his face, although he himself invariably referred to his wife as Mrs Wiggy. He had the reputation of being a martinent and a slave-driver of house physicians. His present houseman was constantly bemoaning how hard he had to work, how his chief was hyper-critical and never satisfied. When he knew that I had applied for the job he constantly regaled me with dreadful forebodings of what was in store for me if I should be appointed.

As the day when the committee that made the house appointment approached, I become more and more apprehensive, fearing that I had put my head into a noose by following my chief's advice. My only comfort was that I had heard that about half a dozen other people had also applied, so perhaps someone else would be appointed and let me off the hook. One Tuesday afternoon as I was presiding at my bougie brigade, the door opened and a colleague popped his head in and said, "I've just heard that you've got Wiggy's job." It was nice of him to let me know, but I suddenly went all tense and the shock of his announcement cost me ten Gold Flake cigarettes. I had read no medicine and seen no medical cases since I had finished swotting for my finals and I seemed to have forgotten it all. The prospect of being in close proximity and under the critical eye of Wiggy filled me with apprehension. How on earth would he react to such a medical ignoramus as myself for a house physician?

As the first day of the new appointment approached, I had decided on my strategy, attack is the best means of defence. At the first opportunity I would inform him myself of my ignorance, and take the wind out of his sails from the start.

On the morning of the day I took up the appointment I stood at the top of the steps at the main entrance to await his arrival, as was customary, all dressed up in my white jacket with a stethoscope sticking out of a pocket.

I watched my new chief as he walked slowly and sedately up the steps apparently lost in thought. As he arrived on the top step I took a deep breath and said, "Good morning, Sir. I am your new house physician. And, Sir, there is one thing I should like to make absolutely clear to you from the start. I don't know my medicine."

He listened to me with his head inclined a little forward and a grave expression on his face. I was feeling pretty awful. When I had said my piece he turned to go into the hospital, as he did so he put a hand lightly on my shoulder, smiled, and said, "I don't know much medicine either. We'll learn a little together during the next six months, won't we?"

Wiggy had won, he had outwitted me, although not in the manner I had expected. I think it must have been his smile that won me over. I walked with him through the entrance hall into the main hospital feeling very different from how I had felt while waiting for him at the top of the steps. Could this man really be the ogre he had been made out to be?

He had an interesting face - handsome, Jewish, sensitive, cultured, although it usually wore a solemn, absorbed, almost withdrawn expression. His smile transformed it, giving it an aura of warmth and affection, with an appealing quality. My fear and apprehension began to evaporate, he seemed to be a very human person.

Gradually as the first few days went by the apprehension I had felt became replaced by affection. Certainly Wiggy could be strict and at times exacting, he involved me in a lot of work. I would go to bed at night pretty tired and late after writing up to date all the patient's case notes ready for his next morning ward rounds. I would write them up sitting in the ward kitchen while the night nurse kept me supplied with cups of tea. I would be up early in the mornings in the ward clinical room doing blood-counts and examining urines, which were some of the chores of a H.P. in those days. I enjoyed working for him, his enthusiasms were so contagious. He took quite a fatherly interest in me, inviting me into his home, a very happy place. He had an extensive private practice, but was no respecter of persons, the humblest of his hospital patients was as important to him as a duchess, not that there were many duchesses in Birmingham, but there were plenty of wealthy business people. It was the fashion in those days for most of the consultants to wear a morning coat and striped grey trousers, but not Wiggy, he always dressed in an ordinary lounge suit with a brightly coloured tie.

During the six months I was his H.P. I came to realise that the actual practice of medicine and the medicine of the text books were poles apart. The text books dealt with diseases. A common saying of Wiggy's was, "I don't treat diseases, I treat people". His reputation amongst the students as a lecturer who could help them pass their examination was not high. He believed that there were basic principles, absent from text books, which had to be learnt.

He used to give a clinical lecture in the hospital one morning each week. I remember that one morning he started the lecture by first staring at the students for a time, and then suddenly announcing, "I always have my bowels well open on Wednesdays. Why?" There was an awed silence amongst the students, the Professor seemed to be such an august and remote figure that they had difficulty in associating him with such a mundane act as defaecation. Then the silence was broken by one brave young student from the back row who hesitatingly said in a low voice, 'You take an aperient on Tuesday evenings." "I never take aperients," replied an indignant Wiggy. Eventually he gave the answer. Wednesday was the day that Punch arrived. Apparently he loved Punch, and every Wednesday morning after breakfast he trotted off to the loo with Punch under his arm.

Now this hadn't taught the students anything that would help them to pass their finals, but they had learnt that the commonest cause of constipation is being in a hurry, and that time and a leisurely mood are necessary for a satisfactory action. They had learnt something which would be of use to them when they became general practitioners and had to give advice to their patients.

Another day he was giving a clinical lecture on the symptoms of poisoning. He suddenly noticed that one of the students was staring out of the window lost in thought and miles away from the symptoms of poisoning. Wiggy pounced on him: "Carey!" he said in a loud voice, 'What are the symptoms of phosphorous poisoning?" Carey was taken aback, he could

15

not bring his mind away from whatever he had been day-dreaming about, possibly some pretty nurse. He tried hard to pull himself together, to think of phosphorous and its possible effects if swallowed. He had to say something, "Luminous stools," he ventured. Wiggy gave him a withering look, then he smiled and said, "That was a flash in the pan, wasn't it?"

What Wiggy was interested in was teaching future doctors practical medicine, not in just filling them up with information that examiners would require of them, they could read that in their books. Thus, his H.P., who had his finals behind him, learnt a lot. He often quoted Sir Robert Hutchison's Litany, which runs as follows:

"From inability to let well alone;
for too much zeal for the new and contempt for the old;
from putting knowledge before wisdom,
and cleverness before common sense;
from treating patients as cases,
and from making the cure of the disease more grievous
than the endurance of the same,
Good Lord deliver us."

I had to carry a copy of the Litany in my pocket, and I still possess it. Although I later became more interested in surgery than in medicine, my six months with Wiggy enabled me to see what was then a new truth in the saying, "a surgeon is a physician who uses his hands." How right my former chief, Billington, had been in giving me the advice he did, and how glad I am that I took it.

Fifty years ago insulin had just been discovered and raw liver was eaten as the treatment of pernicious anaemia. Except for arsenic in the treatment of syphilis there was no chemotherapy, no antibiotics, no cortisone, no anti-depressant drugs. There was no blood transfusion service, no obstetric flying squads, no radio-therapy, medical technology was in its infancy.

What I have written about my time at the Queen's is somewhat nostalgic because they were happy and fulfilling days for me. They belong to an era that will never return. They were the early formative years of one member of a generation of doctors who later had to adapt to the rapid advances in medical science, and to strive to resist the clever subtle indoctrination by amoral drug companies, using insidious advertising methods, making vast profits. Also, mid-way in their professional lives, they were forced to change their whole outlook at the birth of the N.H.S. when the State suddenly, overnight, imposed itself between them and their patients.

Chapter Five

Dick

Dick Tomlins died in February 1928, aged 24. We had been close friends all our student days, had qualified together, and got our first house jobs at the Queen's at the same time. He was a house physician while I was a house surgeon. He was an asthmatic. He got engaged to one of the nurses at the Queen's, but secretly, it would not have done for the Matron to find out, being against the rules for a nurse to be engaged to a student or house-man; she would have had to leave the hospital. They were much in love.

On taking up our house appointments at the Queen's, Dick and I invested in a very ancient car, a Napier, I think it was. It cost £10 and we shared the cost of buying and running it. It was just about on its last legs, the driving seat was high off the ground, it had a dilapidated hood, large brass paraffin lamps, and the steering was stiff and heavy. It used a great deal of oil, and when it was running it belched out dense fumes from the exhaust, so we named it "Flatus". It was anti-socially noisy, but could do 25mph, flat out.

One afternoon Dick took his fiancee out for a run in "Flatus". It grinded to a final halt somewhere on the Lickey Hills. Dick was nearly broke and he knew I was in the same condition, so there was no other possible course than just to abandon poor old "Flatus". Dick pushed it off the road and just left it on the grass verge. As far as I know the rusty remains are still there, but I wish I had it now, it would be worth a bomb.

It was not for another eighteen months that I had a car of my own, I saved up for it. It was a brand new Austin Seven saloon and it cost £105.

Dick's asthma attacks were quite severe. I know that he was allergic to cats because when we did our twenty district midwifery cases as students, he always developed an attack if there was a cat in the house. While he was a house physician he went down with an attack and with a high tempera-ture which persisted. It soon became obvious that he had developed bron-cho-pneumonia , and there was no treatment for that in those days, the sul-phanilamides and antibiotics were years away. He died.

During his illness his secret engagement to the nurse could no longer be hidden from the Matron, who was unexpectedly tolerant, kind and under-standing. She took the nurse off duty so that she could sit by his bedside during the last few days of his life. When Dick died she was shattered.

Philip Harris & Co, was a large pharmaceutical firm in Birmingham. Representatives of the firm called on all the dispensing general practition-ers in the Midlands and beyond. One of them was a chap who had been at King Edward's with me, Stuart Robertson. The Representatives had a friendly relationship with the doctors and knew all about their practices. It was through Stuart Robertson that I learnt about and finally settled down in the Forest of Dean, he knew all the Forest Doctors. Philip Harris & Co. ran a free locom service. A Doctor who wanted a locom tenens when going on holiday, or when suddenly ill, could telephone Philip Harris & Co., who would be able to supply one. Many of the locum tenens were recently qualified doctors who had not yet acquired their own practices, or had a few free weeks between hospital jobs.

About eighteen months after Dick's death, I found I had some free time between jobs, and was anxious to start to earn a little money. The standard locum fee was eight guineas a week plus board and keep and expenses. I rang up Stuart Robertson who put me in touch with an elderly practitioner in Droitwich. I agreed to run his practice for him for a fortnight while he had a holiday.

He lived in a house on the main Birmingham to Worcester road. There were salt mines near, or under, the house, which had caused it to tilt. It looked like a residential truncated Leaning Tower of Pisa. On entering the consulting room the patients had to walk downhill to the doctor's desk. As some of the patients were arthritic visitors taking hydrotherapy at the Droitwich medicinal baths, for which they required a doctor's prescription, they often had difficulty walking on a floor which sloped downwards to the doctor's desk when they had assumed the floor to be level.

I arrived at the doctor's residence the evening before he was due to go on holiday. After a meal he gave me the list of patients that needed visiting and explained the running of his practice. While we were talking there was a ring at the surgery door which he answered. A little later he returned, rummaged in his wife's sewing box, threaded a darning needle with some thread, and told me he wouldn't keep me waiting very long but he had to put some stitches in a chap's arm. Next morning he and his wife departed in an Austin 16 for their holiday leaving the wife's old Austin Seven Tourer for my use.

I dutifully did my best at my first experience of working as a general practitioner. After the morning surgeries, I set off in the Austin 7 to do my list of visits. The first time in my life that I used midwifery forceps was during this locum when I was called in by the District Midwife. The delivery was unexpectedly taking place in the cabin of a canal barge. It was quite an experience.

One morning in the middle of my rounds I was in Fernhill Heath, a village a few miles down the Worcester Road. I turned the car down a side lane and stopped outside a house. I don't know why I stopped, the house was not on the waiting list. I got out of the Austin, walked down the front garden path and knocked on the door.

The door was opened by the Nurse who had been Dick's fiancee at the Queen's. I had not seen her for well over a year. Her home was in Wolverhampton, yet here she was in Fernhill Heath. She greeted me with great surprise and pleasure.

18

"Bill! How good to see you. I've been thinking of you all the morning and wishing I could get in touch with you. I am in great trouble and need some help, and I thought of you. How did you know I was here?" I could not answer, I had not known she was there. She was staying with some friends in the house in Fernhill Heath. To cut a long story short, I was able to give her some help, as she was in dire trouble involving a family crisis.

It was an extraordinary experience. The strange thing was that at the time it all seemed sort of natural to me. It was not until a little later that I realised what an extraordinary experience it was.

I can't explain it, it just happened.

Chapter Six

The Prisoner

He was not my patient and I never spoke to him. But I saw him when I passed his bed. He was operated on by one of the honorary surgeons - never mind which one or at which hospital. He was middle-aged, had a sallow peaky thin face, was going bald, had a sullen look about him and would not look you in the face. He had been admitted to hospital from the local prison, and not for the first time. He had discovered a way to relieve the monotony of prison life by having a couple of weeks in the comfort of a hospital bed. It was very simple, really. He just swallowed things: spoons from the prison kitchen, large screws, pieces of metal, anything he could get hold of that would show on an X-ray photograph.

The surgeon who operated on him to remove the foreign bodies was a rather bumptious, self-opinionated chap who took himself very seriously, regarded himself as above criticism, and was devoid of any sense of humour. He maintained his dignity by dressing in a morning tail-coat, striped grey trousers and a wing collar. He was getting a bit fed up with this jail-bird, especially as he had hinted that the surgeon did not always remove all the objects he had swallowed. As the surgeon was putting the final skin stitches in the incision after removing the various objects from the stomach, he turned to his house surgeon and said in his usual imperious manner:

"First thing tomorrow morning have this man put on a trolley and taken to the X-ray Department. I want an X-ray of his abdomen. I am not letting him go back to prison and swallow another spoon, and then accuse me of having left it behind."

The morning after the operation I met his house surgeon in the main corridor. He had a very broad grin right across his face.

"What's the big joke?" I asked him. "Big joke it is", he replied, "you know that chap from the clink who had swallowed all those things and had them removed yesterday, well he has been X-rayed and the radiographer has just shown me the wet plate. I shall have to wipe this grin off my face before I meet my chief and tell him what it shows, it won't be easy". "Why?" I asked. "Well, he removed all those swollowed foreign bodies alright, but..." I thought he was never going to stop laughing. "But, he's left a pair of artery forceps behind. And he won't think that's funny."

21

Chapter Seven
Beloved Jewel

One morning early in October 1934 I was standing on the deck of the "City of Paris" as it entered Bombay Harbour. Some years has passed since I was at the Queen's. In the interval I had done several senior resident surgical posts, had become a Fellow of the Royal College of Surgeons, and spent three months of study at the London School of Tropical Medicine.

It had been twenty days since the liner had left Liverpool and I was eager to disembark. There had been a short stay at Port Said after which we had passed through the Suez Canal and the Red Sea, and then stopped for a few hours at Port Sudan to discharge some cargo, where I was able to stretch my legs on the edge of the African Continent. It was good to feel the solid earth under my feet again. It had been hot and sticky in the Red Sea with a following wind and a sand storm, at Port Sudan there was a fresh breeze blowing in from the Indian Ocean which I had yet to cross. Now I had crossed it, and straight in front of me was Bombay.

The voyage was over at last although I had 400 miles or so to go by rail to get to my destination. I left Bombay that evening on the Calcutta mail, and stared through the carriage window at the view as the train climbed the Western Ghats on its way to the central Indian Plateau. It was very different scenery from that which I had left behind in England. I reached my destination early the next morning, and as I climbed down from the train I was greeted with "Salaam, Doctor Sahib". I looked down at a diminutive smiling figure who seized my luggage and piled it into the back of an ancient open Chevrolet. That was how I first met Pyare Lal Driver.

Pyare Lal, which being translated means "Beloved Jewel", is a very common name in India. To distinguish himself from all the other Pyare Lals this one had added Driver to his name. For was he not an important personage? He was the motor-driver for the Friends' Hospital in Itarsi, and how could the hospital survive without him? Less than five feet in height he was a much respected figure in Itarsi. That morning I regarded him as just a servant who had been sent to the station to meet me, later he was to become my teacher of many things and my friend.

Itarsi is at a junction where the railway running west-east from Bombay to Calcutta crosses the line running north-south from Delhi to Madras. It was not a large town, before the days of the railway it had been merely a large village. It was set in a rural countryside with the Vindhya Hills to the north and the Satpura range of hills to the south. Those hills were jungle country, Kipling's jungle, somewhat like thickly wooded English parkland, but with huge Banyan trees and pepal and sturdy teak. The trees were alive with rhesus and black-faced monkeys and wild peacocks. Deer abounded, and lurking in the depths were tigers and panthers and the ugly hyenas. It was the homeland of the Gonds, an aboriginal people. Between the two hill ranges flows the wide and sacred Narbada river on its way to the Gulf of Cambay in the Arabian Sea.

On that October morning the monsoon was little more than a month past, from the train the earth looked fresh and green, and there were fields of linseed in bloom making shimmering patches of unbelievable blue. The Mohur Tree, well named the Flame of the Forest, was in flower, giving splashes of the richest crimson I had ever seen. I was to get to know this countryside well, and to discover that it was not always as idyllic as it seemed to me that morning. I was to see it baked brown and parched by a ruthless sun, and turned into quagmires of mud and pools of water by the monsoon rains.

I don't know where Pyare Lal got his training but he was an expert motor mechanic. It was amazing to see what he could do with bits of string and wire to that old Chev, which was really on its last legs, and how he managed to keep it going was a mystery to me. He could take it anywhere in the jungle, driving it with superb self-confidence and skill.

On one day in each week he took me on a tour of branch dispensaries and neighbouring villages. As I sat beside him he taught me some Hindi, although he himself only knew a little English. He enlightened me about local customs, that European ways are not Indian ways. He told me how to address the various personages I had to meet, giving me the background and the gossip about them. When we stopped at a village we were surrounded by a crowd of patients and he would marshall them for me to deal with.

What a conglomeration of diseases I would see: children with protuberant abdomens caused by huge malarial spleens, bodies covered with septic sores and scabies, advanced tuberculosis, tumours of all types and sizes, sore eyes from trachoma, old folk with cataracts, gross deformities from past injuries, and dreadful malnutrition. I felt very inadequate trying to cope with all this suffering with only what I was able to carry in the back of the old Chev. and asking Pyare Lal to try to persuade them to come to the hospital.

I had been in India nearly a year when something unexpected happened. One morning I got a message that Dame Elizabeth Cadbury was at Itarsi Station and was coming to the hospital. She had come off the Calcutta mail as she had been taken ill. She had arrived in Bombay from England the previous day and was on her way to Calcutta to preside over an International Women's Conference.

She was a tall elderly lady very reminiscent of Queen Mary in looks, stature and bearing. When I saw her she looked far from well, with a high temperature and complaining of severe earache. She had a fairly virulent infection of the middle ear, which was unusual in a woman of her age, being a more common condition in children, but it was a condition that could have serious complications.

I found myself suddenly and unexpectedly landed with quite a responsibility as the Dame was an important personage in the Quaker hierarchy. As it happened I had only that week received a supply of a new German drug, Prontosil. Having read some promising reports of its anti-inflammatory properties I had ordered some for use in the hospital but had not yet tried it out. Although I couldn't have known it then, Prontosil was the big breakthrough in chemotherapy, to be followed by the M & B drugs and then by the antibiotics.

In view of the seriousness of her condition and the dire risks of the complications I decided to try it out on the Dame. It was amazing to me how she responded to it, the drug acted immediately. In a few days she was quite well again and anxious to resume her journey. The infection of the middle ear had disappeared as if by magic.

Before she left she told me she was very grateful to the hospital staff for the way they had looked after her, and that she would like to make some little gift to the hospital as a token of her appreciation. I said I would think of something the hospital needed and would let her know before she left.

I then went off and had a big think. The word "little", I decided, when used by someone as wealthy as Dame Elizabeth Cadbury, could be regarded in a fairly broad context. So I went back and told her that what the hospital really needed was a travelling dispensary. She told me to order exactly what was needed and send the bill to her and she would be delighted to pay it.

I designed a body that could be used both as a travelling dispensary and ambulance, with facilities for performing minor operations. It was built by a firm in Calcutta and fixed to a Ford V8 chassis. A few weeks later it arrived by rail at Itarsi station, and Pyare Lal and I went off to fetch it.

Pyare Lal was enraptured; he opened the bonnet and looked at the engine with its eight cylinders, all new and gleaming metal, and his face lit up with happiness. He drove it back to the hospital feeling the power of the engine and comparing it with the old Chev. He later tended and serviced it with absolute devotion; he almost worshipped it, it was always spotlessly clean. He became a wizard at driving and manoeuvring it in the jungle.

It served the villages for many years, long after I had left India. Dame Elizabeth Cadbury did not know the debt she owed to Prontosil. Neither did she know that I had never used Prontosil before, and had treated her as a chocolate guinea pig. From a grub can arise a butterfly. From her ear infection arose blessedness.

One day I removed a huge ovarian cyst. It was put in the sluice room while I finished the remainder of the operations as it was much too large to preserve in a jar, but I wanted to photograph it. When the operating session was over I went to collect it from the sluice room . It was not there. I thought maybe the laboratory boy had taken it to the laboratory, but it was not there either, it had just disappeared. The Lab. boy and I stood on the verandah outside the laboratory discussing the mystery when he suddenly pointed towards the hospital entrance gate.

We saw Pyare Lal riding into the hospital on his bicycle which he was steering with one arm. Underneath his other arm was what looked like an enormous water-melon. It was the missing ovarian cyst. On questioning him it transpired that he had been sitting in a Cafe in the Bazaar talking to some friends, and telling them about the size of the cyst which his hospital had dealt with. His friends had expressed more than some doubt about his story, especially about the size of what had been removed. Pyare Lal had become very indignant and had nipped back to the hospital and fetched the cyst to show to his doubting friends. Pyare Lal was not a man who would tamely submit to having his word doubted.

One of the villages I visited fortnightly, Makoriya, was about ten miles away, along kutcha roads, which had a dispensary with an elderly Indian nurse in charge. A young German from Bavaria, Baron Heinz von Tucker, with his wife and two children lived in a bungalow there. Heinz was an agriculturalist who was endeavouring to help the village folk to increase the yield of their crops. He did a number of interesting experiments, some of them very successful. One of his biggest problems was the conservatism of the villagers who insisted on sticking to their traditional method of cultivation, which yielded poor results.

I remember one time when a lot of damage was being done to their crops by a tribe of monkeys. They did not know how to get rid of them, they could not kill them as they regarded monkeys as sacred animals. So they went along to Heinz and asked him to go into the fields and frighten them away by letting off his gun. They were at pains to explain to him that if by any chance a monkey or two was accidentally shot - well, that was just fate. So Heinz went off and shot the monkeys and everybody was happy.

The nurse at the dispensary assembled all the patients she wanted me to see, and we would take back to hospital those we could persuade to come, piling them and their belongings into the travelling dispensary. One of the villages I called at on the way back had an elderly Mussalman as Headman. He was tall and lean, sported a bushy beard and wore a turban. He always insisted on entertaining me to tea. He would put a handful of tea leaves into a kettle, fill it up with thick buffalo's milk, add a few spices, and put it on a charcoal fire to boil, no water being added. Eventually he would pour the noxious concoction into a drinking vessel and hand it to me. I could not refuse to drink it, it would have hurt the old man's feelings, he was expressing his gratitude for our visit. It was a terrible ordeal for me to get the stuff down. Hot, dusty, sticky and thirsty, I was longing for a long cool drink. However, Pyare Lal seemed to enjoy it.

We visited Makoriya every fortnight alternating with another fortnightly visit, when we set off along a pukka road that heads south into the lower slopes of the Satpura hills, jungle country all the way. About six miles down the road we took a track leading into the forest. Half a mile on we stopped in an open glade and saw a few thatched mud huts and sometimes a tent or two. This was Jamai, in Gond country.

Two Quaker ladies, one elderly from Bristol, Hilda Cashmore, the other young, from Switzerland, Madelaine Jacquier, had started an ashram near

Hoshangabad, about eighteen miles away. Jamai was a small settlement that functioned during the few cool months of the year as a branch of their ashram. The two ladies made periodic visits, sometimes for a few hours, sometimes for a few days. They were investigating the Gond communities, being concerned about what they had heard of their welfare. A resident Indian health worker was attached to the settlement; when we arrived she assembled the patients for me to see under a Pepal tree.

There were about two million Gonds in what was then the Central Provinces, but since independence is now called Madhya Pradash. Before the advent of the British Raj it was called Gondwara - the Kingdom of the Gonds. They are pre-Vedic in origin, having escaped to the hills at the time of the Aryan invasion from beyond North India several thousand years B.C. In the hills they had set up Gond Kingdoms, ruled by Raj Gonds. Hoshangabad, where the local government had its headquarters, was named after the Gond King, Hoshang.

The Gonds prospered for centuries under a loose tribal system until the eighteenth century when they were invaded by the Maratha warriors from the West, and their kingdoms disintegrated. They degenerated into wandering forest tribes. Under British rule they settled down and became cultivators and forest labourers. Before the Maratha invasion they had been prosperous, the Maratha invaders found palaces, reservoirs, quantities of jewellery and jars containing gold coins. Skilled hunters as they were, they were not organised for war.

When I was in India their plight was pitiable. Near Jamai were two brickworks, clay being present in that part of the forest, the Gonds being employed as labourers. The men dug the clay and pressed it into brick moulds. Their daily wage for an eight hour day was 4½ annas, the equivalent of just less than 2p. The women carried the piles of unbaked bricks away on their heads to stack in latticed walls where they could be dried in the sun. Their pay was 3 annas a day.

Large areas of the forest belonged to Landowners (Mulgazars). Most of the Gonds became heavily in debt to the Mulgazars who were also money lenders demanding exorbitant rates of interest. The Gonds were tricked out of their land, the result was that they had become little more than serfs.

The Gonds are animists in religion, peopling the trees, the mountains and the rivers with spirits, adding a few Hindu customs to their animism, their worship of nature. As I drove through the forest I saw the Gond womenfolk, dressed in red saris and tight green bodices, a red caste mark on their foreheads with large white metal anklets that jangled as they walked. They wore beads round their necks, bracelets above the elbow and over their wrists, with small jewels in their noses, gilt studs on their foreheads and gold nails in their teeth. Carrying huge loads of wood on their heads they walked with a regal grace as they picked their way along the jungle paths. The men wore dirty white dhoties and dirty white turbans.

In spite of all their misery and servitude the genetic spirit of their ancestors was still alive inside them. Laughter, song and dance filled their nonworking hours. Their drums could be heard throbbing all through the night as they danced their ancient dances, conjuring up the spirit of the past.

They were lovely people. What will their future be? What is the future for so-called primitive people anywhere as we approach the twenty first century?

After leaving Jamai we returned to the main road and motored another thirty miles. On the way we were repeatedly stopped by small groups of patients who had gathered together waiting for us to appear. Eventually we arrived at a large village called Shahpur where I attended at a large dispensary run by a Swedish Mission to the Gonds. Two kind and industrious Swedish women were in charge, who had lived there many years teaching the Gonds cottage industries. Unlike most missionaries I met, they had a delightful sense of humour, and I enjoyed my visits there.

When we had finished in Shahpur we headed non-stop back to Itarsi. We were on the only metalled road in the district, and Pyare Lal was now in his element, he really made the Ford V8 move. This was his only opportunity of showing what he could do in the way of speed. We would get back to the hospital as the sun was setting, tired and hungry. Pyare Lal would put his beloved bus safely away. I would visit the wards to see how things had been during my absence. As I eventually got back to my bungalow I always found a smiling Pyare Lal waiting patiently for me outside.

"Salaam Sahibji", he would say.

"Salaam Pyare Lal", I would reply.

The smiling Beloved Jewel would then set off for his own home.

Chapter Eight

Lesson From A Primitive

Itarsi is a mushroom town that has grown rapidly around a busy railway junction where the lines from north to south India cross those from west to east. The original village has become submerged and lost. The railway station was a noisy place, with trains constantly coming and going and goods waggons being shunted, the engine drivers blowing their whistles almost continuously, seeming to be playing tunes to each other. It was a cacophony of din and noise. The platforms were crowded with passengers and piles of their luggage, waiting sometimes for many hours for their connections, many lying fast asleep on the platform. Others were squatting in groups, smoking, or chewing pan, spitting the red juice onto the ground. There was a diversity of multi-coloured people. Bearded and turbanned Sikhs. Moslem women with their faces veiled and wearing trousers, or covered by a black veil from head to toe with a small net at eye-level. There were Hindu women in gaily coloured saris, demurely hiding their faces in the folds. A few Indians worse European dress. Many of the men wore white Gandhi caps. All the social groups in India were congregated here, from the Untouchables to the Brahmans and the wealthy cultured Parsees in their silks. The coolies were squatting in groups gossiping and sharing a bidi (an Indian cigarette) which they passed round, each taking a draw through cupped hands without it touching their lips. They rushed about the platform shouting at the tops of their voices when a train arrived. Mingling with the passengers were vendors of sweets, cigarettes and pan which were laid out on a tray suspended by string around their necks. Itarsi was a very noisy place. The noise increased at sundown when added to the noise from the Bazaar and the railway station was the beating of drums and gongs putting the Gods to sleep.

Leading North from Itarsi is the road to Hoshangabad ten miles away, it is not a jungle road, on either side are fields of wheat, lentils, millet and linseed. A mile or two before the town is reached there is a large outcrop of rocks on which are pre-historic paintings of deer and hunters on horseback. Local Government had its Headquarters in Hoshangabad and the Deputy Commissioner had his residence there. It was a quiet, sleepy, unhurried town, very different from Itarsi. It had remained almost unchanged through centuries, unlike Itarisi it had roots and traditions. It is situated on the banks of the sacred Narbada river, three quarters of a mile wide. The centre of the town is Budni Ghat, wide stone steps leading down to the river where men and women are bathing. Women wash their

28

clothes, beating them on the stone steps, while others hold up their saris, unfurled for the sun and wind to dry them. At the top of the steps are ancient Hindu temples, with a few wandering sadhus, their faces smeared with white ashes, squatting outside. At the entrance to the temples are stone bulls and linguas garlanded with marigolds. But the best time to see the town is at night during the autumn festival, Devali (festival of lights). All the houses, shops and temples are illuminated by myriads of tiny lights from lamps consisting of wicks immersed in oil in small earthenware saucers. Hoshangabad is a country town, a sort of Indian Tunbridge Wells, while Itarsi is more like an Indian version of Crewe.

It was an unwritten rule in India, when hunting from a machan which is a wooden platform in a tree, not to go after a wounded tiger until it is daylight. Soon after I took over Itarsi hospital two English army officers built a machan in the jungle some miles away from us. They tethered a goat near the base of a tree and climbed onto the platform and waited, hoping that later a tiger would come along, attracted by the bleating of the goat.

After the moon had risen they saw a tiger creeping stealthily towards the goat. One of the officers fired at it and hit it. Excitedly he slithered down the tree to inspect the kill, but the tiger had not been killed, only wounded, and it mauled him terribly. His companion managed to finish off the tiger, and eventually to get the severely injured man to hospital. He was in a very bad state and died a few hours after admission.

His friend was badly shaken by what had happened. He stayed with us for a few days making the necessary arrangements and writing to the bereaved parents in England. I later received a letter from them thanking the hospital for what we had done for their son. Unfortunately there had been very little we did or could have done. They kindly enclosed a cheque as a donation to the hospital.

The beds in the hospital, except in the European ward, were charpoys, made of wood and rope, and appeared to me as being very unsuitable to nurse patients on. I used the donation to buy a Fowler bed, thinking it would be a good start in modernising the hospital. We bought one from a surgical firm in Bombay. The first patient we put in it was a Gond who was very ill suffering from an empyema following pneumonia.

Empyema is a condition in which the chest on one side becomes filled with several pints of thick creamy pus which causes the lung to collapse. The treatment consisted of removing a few inches of a rib and inserting a wide rubber tube into the empyema cavity to drain away the pus and allow the collapsed lung to re-expand. This was done early one morning. It was an ideal case to nurse on a Fowler bed, so he was taken back to the Ward from the Theatre and propped up in a satisfactory position on the brand new Fowler bed.

I went on working during the rest of the morning and when I had finished I went along to see how the Gond patient was getting on. I entered the Ward and looked at the Fowler bed. It was empty. The patient was curled up fast asleep underneath it, and refused to be put back in it, becoming very agitated when we tried to persuade him. It was obvious that he was frightened of it. For the remainder of his stay in Hospital, he was nursed on the floor. He made an uninterrupted recovery and returned to his village fit and well.

I had learnt my first important lesson. Although an English Doctor trained in English Hospitals, I was now in India, up-country, living amongst simple Indian village folk. I realised that it was I who must do the adjusting, and not impose my western standards on them. A primitive tribesman had taught me a lesson. The charpoys remained in the hospital, they were what the patients were used to, not European beds with spring mattresses.

Chapter Nine

Wycliffe and Priti Bhai

The Laboratory in the Hospital was a good sized room. It had been organised by one of my predecessors, Dr. Robert John Gittins, but had not been used for two or three years before I took over. Robert Gittins became the Pathologist at the Childrens Hospital, Birmingham, after he returned from India, a few years before I went there. Unfortunately he and his six year old son Christopher were drowned in the River Severn in a boating accident in 1934. Christopher had fallen out of the boat and Robert dived into the River in an attempt to rescue him. When their bodies were recovered Robert had his son in his arms.

I never regretted the three months I spent at the London School of Tropical Diseases. It is impossible to run a hospital efficiently in India without a laboratory. The work involved in it was very time consuming, and I soon realised that somehow I must get the services of a Laboratory Technician. I mentioned this one day to Heinz when I was visiting the Makoriya Dispensary. He told me of a particularly bright lad in the village who had been away to High School and had just finished his education. Agricultural work did not appeal to him, neither did clerical work, but he had been interested in scientific subjects at school. I had a talk with the lad and was very impressed by his intelligence and character. He spoke excellent English, was tall and slim, and very good looking. He belonged to a Christian family which I think originally must have been of Brahman stock before being rescued by the Quakers during the dreadful famines of the 1860's. His name was Wycliffe. Why on earth an Indian village baby boy should be given the name of Wycliffe is beyond me.

I arranged for him to come to the hospital to work in the laboratory. Before very long he could make a better blood-film than I could, and had learnt to stain and identify the malaria parasite in a red corpuscle, and to identify amoebic cysts and the ova of intestinal parasites. Within a few months he was a very efficient and reliable laboratory technician.

Wycliffe was a hard worker. The time he worked his hardest was when we had a serious cholera epidemic in the district. Cholera is a dreadful disease, a man can loose so much fluid and salts from his body that he rapidly becomes dehydrated and may die in a few hours. The only treatment is to replace the fluids and salts intravenously, several pints being needed by each patient.

The solution had to be prepared and sterilised, this was Wycliffe's job. For several weeks an Indian assistant doctor and I worked in alternative

31

six-hour shifts, infusing patients who were pouring up to the hospital. There was a queue of bullock carts up the road outside containing cholera victims, most of them moribund on arrival, many must have died on the way. It was wonderful to watch a dehydrated near-corpse gradually come back to life as the fluid ran into his veins. Wycliffe kept us supplied with the solution. I don't know how many gallons he must have prepared. When he ate and when he slept I just don't know, he did not leave the laboratory during the epidemic.

We managed to keep the epidemic out of the hospital compound. Everyone employed was inoculated with anti-cholera vaccine. Nobody was allowed in who had not been inoculated. Pyare Lal was also kept busy taking workers to the villages to permanganate the wells and male nurses to inoculate the villagers. Everybody worked hard, nobody grumbled, but we were all pretty exhausted by the time the epidemic was over.

The only accolade I received was a letter from a very indignant Quaker woman in England, protesting that a member of the Society of Friends should encourage vivisection by inoculating innocent Indian peasants with a vaccine. She was ignorant of the fact that animals are not used in the preparation of the vaccine. She was also ignorant and unimaginative of what an un-inoculated innocent peasant looked like when suffering from cholera.

The senior nurse was a charming and attractive girl called Priti Bhai, very efficient at her work. The Indian nurses lived in small groups in little houses in a part of the compound behind the English sister's bungalow. They did their own cooking and looked after themselves. The male nurses, called compounders, were non-resident. Priti Bhai, being the senior nurse, was given a little house of her own. Wycliffe fell in love with her, and she with him.

One evening he was seen coming out of her house. They had been unchaperoned. The balloon went up! The Sister had earmarked Priti Bhai for a life of nursing and perpetual spinsterhood like unto herself. Priti Bhai had been an orphan brought up by an American mission. The Sister took upon herself the role of parent and refused to let her marry Wycliffe. I remarked that I thought their marriage would be a very pleasant event to happen in the hospital. She replied that when she saw Wycliffe leaving Priti Bhai's house she felt physically sick. I could not resist replying that I felt sorry for anyone who felt like that because two very attractive people were in love with each other. Fortunately we later got two Sisters with very different outlooks.

Strings were pulled behind the scenes and in a week or two, Wycliffe's parents married him off to another girl, quite a nice girl, and probably suitable in their eyes.

A few days after Wycliffe's wedding, I was walking across the compound when I heard screams and shouts for help coming from some nurses outside their quarters. I hurried over to find Priti Bhai with her sari in flames. I rolled her in some matting to quench the flames, and she was admitted to hospital. Her face, neck, shoulders and arms were badly burnt. They took a long time to heal, after which poor Priti Bhai was no longer beautiful. The scars and contractions of the skin of her face and neck had disfigured her terribly.

She had explained the cause of the accident as having been due to her sari catching alight as she was bending over the fire while cooking a meal. I expect that is what happened, it is a common enough event in Indian homes, the fire-place being on the ground. But the timing worried me, the accident happening just after Wycliffe's marriage. I wondered whether deep down in the collective unconscious of Priti Bhai's mind there was not some atavistic or archetype urge related in some way to suttee, or whether it was an example of Jung's synchronicity. For many centuries Indian women had accepted suttee until the British made it illegal early in the nineteenth century. Perhaps I was being too fanciful and too much influenced by Jung's writings.

When Priti Bhai's burns had healed I was informed one day that she had been sent back to the American mission where she had been brought up. I never saw her again, nor did Wycliffe.

Chapter Ten

Blood and Mr Rhao

English was a subject that was taught in all the Middle and High Schools in India. The curriculum included the learning of English proverbs. Just as some Hindi words have found their way into the English language, like pyjama, char, posh, so some English words found their way into Indian conversation. Some of these, particularly certain adjectives, were picked up from British soldiers stationed in India. Occasionally the slang of the British Tommy got mixed up with the proverbs learnt at school. One man, writing to tell me of the death of his wife, informed me that "the hand that rocked the cradle has kicked the bucket".

Those who lived up-country and could speak English regarded themselves as elevated into the ranks of the "educated", such a one was Mr Rhao. He preferred the English "Mr." to the Indian "Shri". He considered himself emancipated and westernised. He was a guard employed by the Grand Indian Peninsular Railway Company. He was an extrovert, a flamboyant individual who relished anything suggestive of the melodramatic. He loved showing off his command of the English language to any Englishman he might meet.

One day we admitted his wife into hospital in a critical condition. She had an internal haemorrhage from a ruptured tubal pregnancy, and had lost a lot of blood. We operated and dealt with the bleeding, but I feared we had been too late to save her life. In England she would have been given a blood transfusion. I explained all this to Mr Rhao who responded by flinging wide his arms in a dramatic gesture, saying "If only she could have some of mine". This was too good a possible opportunity to miss, so I seized his arm and marched him off to the laboratory. I pricked his thumb to get a drop of blood for grouping, and as luck would have it, he was a universal donor. On cross matching with his wife's blood I found to my relief that it was compatible. Mr Rhao was getting somewhat bemused by all this. I persuaded him to lie down on a couch, I put a tourniquet on his arm, inserted a French's needle into his basilic vein and drew off one and a half pints of his blood into an oxalate solution. I then went over to the ward and transfused it into his wife. It made all the difference to her condition, she rallied and made an excellent recovery.

It took only a little time for Mr Rhao to recover from the surprise that his dramatic fantasy-gesture had been turned into a reality. He was overjoyed about his wife's recovery but especially about being the hero who had saved her life by donating his blood. For the next three months he wore an enormous wad of gamgee tissue bandaged onto his elbow to protect the prick in the skin caused by the French's needle.

He often popped round to my bungalow for a chat, usually when I was particularly busy. On one such occasion he appeared to be full of indignation about something. It transpired that he had written to the G.I.P Railway Authorities informing them of how he had given his blood and saved his wife's life. He had suggested to them that this noble action warranted a rise in his salary. The G.I.P. Railway Authorities had turned down his suggestion and he was very incensed about it. Travelling up and down the line at his work he would tell all and sundry about the transfusion, displaying his bandaged elblow. It was quite a good public relations exercise as far as the hospital was concerned, it was a breakthrough I was needing. On a number of occasions previously I had appealed in vain for a donor, but it had seemed too mysterious a performance for anyone to volunteer. Mr Rhao had demonstrated what a blood transfusion could do and that it was a harmless procedure.

Living in Itarsi was a venerable elderly Mohemmedan who was the only Moslem in the town who had made the pilgrimage to Mecca. He was therefore held in high esteem in the town as a holy man and automatically became the head of the Moslem community. His name was Harjiji. I approached him with the suggestion that his fraternity could provide blood donors for the hospital. Harjiji was not going to be outdone by Rhao, a Hindu. He rounded up a number of Moslem young men and brought them along to the hospital. We grouped them all, making a list of the universal donors, and gave the list of names to Harjiji. After that all I needed to do when I wanted a pinit of blood for a patient was to send a message to Harjiji. He consulted the list of names and using his religious authority turned up with a not always particularly willing volunteer donor. They gave their blood to any patient, irrespective of religion. It was often a good practical exercise in Hindu-Moslem-amity. I think this was probably the first blood transfusion service in India, certainly in rural India.

Chapter Eleven

The Mahatma

Living in India I tried to adjust myself to Indian customs although there were some things I found difficult to accept and could not bring myself to condone. I could make allowances for the many Indian superstitions, we have many of our own back home. The extremes of poverty, and the greed and extortion and power of the landlords and money lenders were a different matter. So was the caste system and the deplorable plight of the Untouchables. Trying to diet a caste Hindu was very difficult, indeed impossible, when the relatives cooked the food and I had no control. Then one day I thought of Gandhi, the champion of the Untouchables, who had renamed them the Harijans, the "Children of God". I remembered what a Congress worker in the town had told me, that Gandhi's principal enemy was not the British Raj, but the caste system. So I wrote to Gandhi, telling him of my problem of controlling a caste patient's diet, and I asked him if he had any suggestions to offer. A few days later I received a post card from him saying "Come and talk with me", and giving me an appointment.

I read Gandhi's post card with considerable surprise. I did not really know what I had expected in reply to my letter, which I had written on impulse. Sevagram village where he had his ashram was about 275 miles away. An ashram is a religious retreat for communal living, surely an Englishman would feel out of place there. Those who visited Gandhi were people of importance, politicians from England and the leaders of the Indian Congress. India was in a very interesting condition politically at that time, why on earth should Gandhi want to spend some of his time talking to a doctor running a hospital in a remote part of India who had nothing whatsoever to do with politics? Not to keep the appointment he had so kindly sent would appear ill-mannered. I must confess that I was intrigued by the prospect of meeting Gandhi personally, I had heard and read so many conflicting reports about him, so I decided to accept his invitation.

I felt rather self-conscious as I kicked off my sandals on entering Gandhi's house, which was identical with all the houses in the poverty-stricken village nearby. It was made of mud bricks with a thatched roof and an earthen floor, and consisted of one room with a small verandah. My immediate impression was how ugly Gandhi seemed, but in a few seconds that impression completely vanished. He was sitting on the floor dealing with some papers on his desk, which was an upturned wooden box on which was imprinted the words "Lifebuoy Soap". He wore a dhoti, his legs were bare, and a shawl over his shoulders partially covered his naked chest. He was wearing steel spectacles, fastened to his dhoti with a large safety pin was a big tin watch; at his side was a spinning wheel. I noticed that hanging on the wall was a small picture of Christ. He looked at me for a while with piercing eyes, then he smiled and asked me to sit down, which I did, on the floor.

I do not know what I had expected, but this was no "Naked fakir"as Winston Churchill had dubbed him. He started the conversation by asking me about the hospital and its problems, and they were practical questions. I explained the difficulties over diet. He remarked that the caste system was a curse from which Hinduism needed to cleanse itself. Next he started talking about the Society of Friends, saying that there were several Quakers who were his special friends. He gave a chuckle and told me a story about what happened when he had been in London attending the Round Table Conference. Some Quaker worthies had invited him to one of their meetings for worship. He was told, he said, that they were held in silence and that all he needed to do was to relax. He chuckled again, and told me that he had been exhausted after the long hours at the Conference. "I must confess", he said, "that I relaxed too much. I slept all through the hour of silence. That sleep did me a lot of good".

Having heard sentimental descriptions from some of the worthies who had been present at that Meeting, and been told by them of how Gandhi's face had been illuminated and transfigured by adoration during the act of worship, I could not help grinning. Gandhi watched me as I grinned. It suddenly dawned on me that by watching my response to his story he was weighing me up.

We talked of other things during which I referred to him as being a pacifist. "I am not a pacifist", he said, "I am a non-violent activist". He was very easy to talk to, he was direct and sincere, full of common sense, and humour that was almost puckish, a very loveable man.

We talked for about three quarters of an hour, when his Secretary Mahadev Desai, came along to break off the interview. As I got up to leave Gandhi said he would like to help me with the problem of dieting caste Hindus. He promised to write me a letter in Hindi with an English translation. I was to hang up a copy of the Hindi version in a prominent position in the hospital. I thanked him and left with Mahadev Desai.

A few days after I returned to Itarsi I received the letter, we hung it up on the Outpatient Verandah. Groups of patients and their relatives and friends could very often be seen clustered around it in animated discussion and argument. The letter read as follows:

With reference to your hospital scheme, which you were good enough to explain to me today, you tell me that you propose to add more family quarters for your patients' families who would desire to supply the patients with food prepared by them.

My experience, in what little hospital work I have done, has shown me that it is a harmful concession to prejudice. For, the food cooked by private parties, is rarely cooked according to directions. Doting relatives disregard restrictions, pamper patients, and retard recovery where their false affection does not prove fatal to the patients.

I would, therefore, strongly advise you, for the sake of the patients themselves, not to encourage private cooking for patients under your care, even as you would not allow relatives to administer to them drugs of their own choice.

If the patients bring families, they can see the former only at stated times and under proper restrictions.

I know that there are, unfortunately, so called higher castes, who observe untouchability as to food. In my opinion you cannot afford to pander to such prejudices, especially at a time when untouchability is fast dying.

What I hope you will do is to run a strictly vegetarian kitchen for those who would not on any account take flesh meat or fish.

Yours sincerely,

M.K. Gandhi."

There had been a meeting of the Congress Working Committee with Gandhi the day before I visited him. Mahadev Desai took me along and introduced me to those who had not yet left. I remember that I met Jawaharlal Nehru; Rajendra Prasad; Sarojini Naidu and Jaya Prakash Narayan. I also met Aryanaykham and his wife Asha Devi who were in charge of the basic education programme. These had all been in prison for their political activities, some of them several times. What surprised me was with what affection they regarded England and English people. They seemed to have no bitterness or animosity, it was only the political system they were against. They did not know who I was or why I was there, yet they treated me with the greatest friendliness, because I was English. Nehru particularly had a long talk with me, and asked if he could visit me next time he passed through Itarsi. His wife had died some years previously from tuberculosis contracted while in jail.

Mahadev Desai then handed me over to the care of two ashram workers: Jogneshwar Gogoi, a young Assamese, and Herbert Fischer, a tall blonde young German, a fugitive from Hitler's Gestapo. Not long afterwards, with Gandhi's consent, they both left Sevagram ashram and came to work with me at the hospital as social workers amongst the patients' families.

Those who may read these reminiscences will know the name of Gandhi, and may have seen Richard Attenborough's splendid film but may not know much about him. A great deal has been written of his life, sometimes in great detail, sometimes objectively, sometimes critical, sometimes sentimental. In order to identify himself with the poor of India he had renounced all personal possessions and wore a peasant's loin cloth. He was in his mid-sixties when I visited him. Being human, Gandhi had faults and made mistakes. There were times when he could be a little vain, times when he could be unreasonably obstinate, or autocratic. He was narrow minded over some matters, his views on sex-bramacharya (complete abstinence of sex even with marriage) were unnatural. As Bapu, the father of the nation, he was superb; as a father to his own sons he was a failure. His wife, Kasturbhai, sometimes had a lot to put up with. Yet he was loved by all around him, and worshipped and adored by four hundred million people, who would kneel down and kiss the ground on which his feet had trod, as I have seen. During his lifetime he received the greatest honour that India could give to one of her sons; he was proclaimed a Mahatma - "a Great Soul".

Gandhi, who greatly admired the British, considered it was immoral for them to govern India. With him it was more a matter of morals than of politics. He became determined that it must be ended after the massacre at Jallianwallah Bagh in Amritsa in 1919. General Dyer, with crass stupidity and callousness, ordered troops to open fire on a crowd of 6,000 unarmed men, women and children who had assembled to celebrate a religious festival after he had banned public demonstrations. According to police reports 379 people were killed and many were wounded. The world was shocked. For the remainder of his life Gandhi fasted on the day of the anniversary of the massacre.

Gandhi resolved to free India from British domination, without resorting to violence. He founded an ashram at Sabarmati on the banks of the Sabarmati river just outside the city of Ahmedabad in Gujerat Province. From there he preached Satyagraha - non-violence. He started a campaign of non-cooperation with the British Raj. He instituted the Khadi (homespun) movement, English cloth was boycotted. The people were encouraged to spin and weave their own cloth, and only wear Khadi clothes. The spinning wheel became the symbol of free India, and today it is incorporated in the Indian national flag.

At the ashram he trained satiagrahis - men and women dedicated to non-violence. It takes considerable self-discipline to practice satyagraha, to offer no resistance whatever to physical violence. Gandhi taught that it had a spiritual basis, calling it "Soul Force". Strict training was necessary to become a satiagrahi.

By 1930 he had decided that the time had come for swaraj (self government). He wrote to the Viceroy, Lord Irwin, demanding it, saying that should it be refused he would start a nationwide non-cooperation movement, but pledging it to non-violence. Lord Irwin, one of the best of India's Viceroys, was a deeply religious and sincere man, he replied to Gandhi in a quiet tone, pointing out that Gandhi's action would inevitably become involved in conflict with the law.

It was illegal in those times for Indians to manufacture salt or collect it where it was naturally deposited. Salt was a government monopoly protected by the Salt Law. Salt was an essential ingredient to the Indian's diet. This was the law that Gandhi decided to break.

In March 1930 he set forth on his famous salt march. He walked from the Sabarmati ashram to Dandi on the sea coast, a distance of 240 miles. Clad only in his dhoti and with a bamboo staff he walked ten to fifteen miles a day at the head of a procession. He started with about eighty volunteers, but as he marched the procession grew in numbers, hundreds joining daily. By the time he reached Dandi on April 5th the procession was two miles long, and the authorities became alarmed. The night of April 5th was spent in prayer, and next morning in full view of everybody Gandhi broke the law.

He stooped down and picked up a lump of salt and held it aloft. He had challenged the British Empire with a handful of salt!

For a few days the Authorities did nothing. But all across India people started breaking the Salt Law, and were picketing the liquor shops, which was illegal, as they were government owned. There were public demonstrations of burning of English cloth. The Authorities decided that the time had come for them to act with a show of strength. Gandhi was arrested. The satiagrahis had been well trained, not one retaliated. They were beaten to the ground by the police who became more and more frenzied as wave upon wave of non-resisting satiagrahis advanced towards them, only to be beaten unresisting to the ground, the beatings going on for two hours.

This attack, coupled with Gandhi's arrest, only made the situation in the country worse. All over India there were protest meetings, strikes and anti-British demonstrations. Lord Irwin, who respected Gandhi, was forced into a position against his will of using massive repression. Men and women were arrested in their thousands until the prisons were full to overflowing. Then the Viceroy sent for Gandhi.

In February 1931 Gandhi, clad only in his dhoti, with bare legs and naked chest, walked up the steps of the Viceregal House. He was shown into Lord Irwin's study, and the two men talked together for several hours. When Gandhi left the Viceroy himself accompanied him to the door, saying, "Good night, Mr Gandhi, and my prayers go with you". There were several more conversations between these two deeply religious men who held each other in mutual respect. The outcome was the promise of a Round Table Conference in London to discuss Indian Independence, and a repeal of the Salt Law. Gandhi then called off the civil disobedience movement.

The Round Table Conference met in London from September to December 1933, but nothing came out of it. Gandhi returned to India to find that the Viceroy, Lord Irwin, had been replaced by Lord Willingdon, a hard-liner. Gandhi was arrested a few days after his return and imprisoned without trial.

A few months later the British Government announced a Communal Award which involved a separate electorate for the Untouchable Community of sixty million persons. Gandhi maintained that this would perpetuate their state of untouchability. He wanted a revolutionary change of heart by the Hindus, so that they could welcome the Harijans back into the Hindu fold. In jail he started a "fast unto death" against the Communal Award. Within a few days a miracle had happened, all over India the

Untouchables were being welcomed into Hindu temples without restriction. The British Government agreed to a compromise to be incorporated into the Communal Award. Gandhi, now very close to death, broke his fast and there was rejoicing all over India that he had not died.

But he had not won. A week after he broke his fast, the strict orthodox wing of the Hindu community forced the temples to close their doors once more against the Untouchables. Dr Ambedkar, who claimed to be the leader of the Untouchables, insisted that they were a separate community.

When Gandhi was released from prison in 1934 he announced that he was resigning from politics and that India would only be truly free when the half million villages were freed from poverty. He closed the ashram at Sabarmati and started a new one at Sevagram, where I visited him. It was a village of poverty-striken Untouchables.

Gandhi started to try and free the village from its poverty and illiteracy. He showed them how to improve their houses, he started a school, built latrines for them, and every morning he swept the village street himself hoping to shame the villagers into using the latrines. He started village industries - spinning, weaving, paper-making, and other crafts. When I visited him three years later on my first of several visits it was amazing what had been achieved. It was by then an active colony of workers, with a school for training teachers in basic education, and social workers learning village crafts. Although he had announced that he had retired from politics there was a steady stream of Congress Leaders visiting him for discussions and to ask his advice. Then came the second World War, and for most of it Gandhi and the Congress Leaders were in jail again.

When World War Two was over a Labour Government was returned to power in Britain. Clement Atlee, the Prime Minister, decided that the time had come for India to be given Independence within the British Commonwealth. He sent out as Viceroy Lord Louis Mountbatten, who during the war was Commander-in-Chief of the South East Asia Command.

An interim government was installed with Jawaharlal Nehru as Prime Minister. This did not please the power-seeking Mohamed Ali Jinna, head of the Moslem League, who boycotted it. He insisted that a separate Moslem State, Pakistan, should be created. Nehru did not agree and Gandhi was completely opposed to it. Jinnah announced that August 15th, 1946, would be "Direct Action Day", but nobody understood what he meant. As August 15th dawned they understood; the Mohammedans attacked the Hindus, killing them in their thousands; men, women and children. Three days later in Bengal and Bihar State the Hindus retaliated, murdering Moslems.

Gandhi, now 77 years old, was stricken with grief by what had happened. He set off to visit the affected villages, appealing for the slaughter to be stopped. Then he set up a camp in a Mohammedan village stating that he would stay there until his death or until the killings stopped. He went on a "half-fast", eating a minimum of food. After a month, when Gandhi was emaciated and near to death, the killings stopped. Then when he had recuperated, he spent several months walking from village to village appealing for peace between Hindu and Moslem.

While he was away in Bengal, the Congress, the Muslim League and the Viceroy were dividing up India. Lord Mountbatten sent for Gandhi to consult him and ask his advice. Gandhi was adamant that India should not be partitioned, he considered that it was not the solution; but nobody agreed with him.

On the 15th August 1947, (one year after Jinnah's "Direct Action Day"), the Viceroy handed over power to two new countries, India and Pakistan. Gandhi was nearly broken hearted, not only by the dismemberment of his Mother India, but that his colleagues and friends of so many years had agreed to it. It was not unnatural for them to be tempted by the power that hanged so close and tantalizingly before them. They let Jinnah have his way, they had waited long and suffered much so that the destiny of India should be in their hands.

Whoever drew the boundary lines between the two new states must have been incredibly stupid. Two Pakistans were created, West Pakistan and East Pakistan (now Bangladesh). They were over a thousand miles apart, with nothing in common except their religion. They had different languages, different origins, cultures and traditions.

The boundary line also cut the Punjab, the home of the Sikhs, in half. The sikhs regarded the Moslems as their traditional enemies. Suddenly half of them finding themselves inside, and a part of, a Moslem nation, revolted; they started slaughtering Mohammedans. This spread, and the Hindus and Mohammedans began murdering each other and soon the whole of the Punjab was in chaos.

The Viceroy sent in 50,000 troops to restore order, but they failed. 300,000 people were murdered and 14 million people fled from their homes, Hindus from Pakistan and Moslems to Pakistan. Next, similar trouble flared up in Bengal. This time Lord Mountbatten did not send troops, he sent Mahatma Gandhi, "My one-man police force" he called him. This frail old man set forth and walked across Bengal, a bamboo staff in one hand and leaning the other on the shoulder of Manu, his favourite grand-daughter, and at once the killings stopped.

When he returned to Delhi he discovered that the new Indian and Pakistani Governments were quarelling over 40 million pounds that legally belonged to Pakistan but which was in India's hands, and India had refused to hand over the money. Gandhi declared it a debt of honour and that it must be paid. Still the Indian Government refused to pay, so Gandhi started a "fast unto death"; it was his twentieth and last fast. The Indian Government remained obstinate, but on the third day of the fast Nehru handed over the money and India kept her honour.

It was too much for the extreme orthodox conservative wing of the Hindu community that Gandhi should fast on behalf of Mohammedans. They plotted to kill him, and threatening letters were sent. On the 26th of January, 1948, two bombs were thrown into the compound where he was staying. Two days later, as he was walking to his daily prayer meeting, a fanatical Hindu youth walked up to him and shot him three times in the chest. Gandhi fell dying to the ground whispering "Rama, Rama", the Hindu name for God. He died with the name of God on his lips.

India suffered an awful shock, and was plunged into grief, remorse and shame that this should have happened to their beloved Bapu whom they loved and revered. His body was turned to ashes on a funeral pyre which was attended by several million of his people who came to pay homage and show their grief.

This is a very brief resume of Gandhi's life, but there is so much more I could write. I have made no mention of his twenty-two years in South Africa where his conception of satagraha took place. I have tried to show a few of the high peaks in his life, to give an impression of the man and the spirit that moved him. It is a true story of a Hindu from a remote part of India who demonstrated to the world what love and non violence could do.

Gandhi challenged the might of the British Empire by holding aloft a handful of salt. One is reminded of that Man in Galilee, a Jew, who challenged the might of the Roman Empire with love and non violence. Who held up before thousands of his hungry, suffering and oppressed people, who had come in their thousands to make him their warrior-king, not a pinch of salt, but five loaves and two small fishes. And he died a violent death.

Chapter Twelve

Herbert and Jug

Disease and poverty go hand in hand. Patients were coming into hospital, were getting cured, and then returning to the same condition which had often been responsible for the disease in the first place.

I discussed this problem with the two ashram workers, Herbert Fischer and Jogneshwar Gogoi during my visit to Sevengram ashram. We decided that, subject to Gandhi's approval, they should join me in Itarsi, as Social Workers. A few days after I returned from Sevegram Herbert turned up.

He was a very tall, blonde, handsome German, with a fine physique. He belonged to a Moravian family back in Germany. He had not joined the Hitler Youth Movement, and later had refused to do military service under the Nazis. He had managed to slip out of Germany just in time, with the Gestapo at his heels. He then hitch-hiked all the way to India finishing up in Gandhi's ashram. Making his way across India he had been appalled at the poverty he had seen. He had come to the conclusion that the only way to raise the standard of living of the peasants was to create co-operative producing societies. I agreed with him that we should try this out in the district around Itarsi. Before attempting this we decided that we should have a look at what was being done in this way in other parts of India.

We knew that Rabindranath Tagore, the Bengali Poet, had instituted a co-operative village adjoining his University at Shantineketan, in Bengal. We had also heard of Sir Daniel Hamilton's co-operatives at Gosaba in the Sunderbans, so we decided that we should visit these two places. We worked out that from Itarsi to Shantineketan, and then to Gosaba, and back to Itarsi, involved travelling 1,870 miles. To travel that distance as Europeans would cost far too much, so we decided to travel 3rd class, eat only Indian food, and never spend more than 4 annas on a meal.

Third class was really fourth class, as the G.I.P. Railway had 1st class, 2nd class, inter class and 3rd class. It was the cheapest way to travel. Our carriage held over forty passengers and was very over-crowded. Each group of people had brought large quantities of bundles, bedding, pots and pans, to say nothing of swarms of babies and children. They all talked in loud voices to drown the noise of the train. The seats were hard wooden benches. The lavatory was just a⁻ hole in the floor with no washing facilities, to reach it involved clambering over piles of luggage and crawling children. Sleep was impossible, as there was no room to lie down. It was not a very comfortable journey.

We arrived at Shantineketan tired, dirty and dishevelled. A Guest House was available for visitors and a polite Bengali showed us to our rooms and said he would make arrangements for us to be shown around next day. He asked us our names, Herbert said "Dr Tandy and Mr Fischer". About half an hour later he returned and said the Poet would be pleased to have tea with us next day. We had a bath, slept well, and next day were taken over to the Poet's house. Tagore was very disappointed to discover that I was not a Doctor of Literature, not even a Doctor of Philosophy, but just a philistine sawbones. He was friendly and courteous, but our interview was brief.

We were disappointed with what we saw at Shantineketan, there was an artificiality about the place. It gave us the impression of being a rather over-heated hot-house of Bengali Art and Culture, revolving around the central figure of the Poet. It was all rather wealthy Bengali upper middle class. Alright, I suppose, in a way, but it was making no contribution to the relief of the suffering of the Indian masses. It was not our cup of tea. The model co-operative village, Shrinketan, appeared to be a show piece, with handicrafts quite unsuitable for the poor peasants around Itarsi, and was rather arty-crafty. We did not think we could learn anything from it, so we decided not to overstay our somewhat subdued welcome, and set off on our visit to Gosaba in the Sundarbans.

The Sundarbans are a collection of islands in the Ganges Delta. They are malaria infested jungles intersected by streams of brackish water, inhabited mainly by tigers and crocodiles and some wandering fishermen. Gosaba was one of these islands, situated fifty miles south-east of Calcutta, about 22,000 acres in size. We arrived in Calcutta from Shrinketan and took a train from there to a place whose name I have forgotten where there is a jetty where we could get a small steamer for Gosaba. We arrived there in the evening a few minutes after the boat had left. It would not return for twelve hours, so we got into our sleeping bags and spent the night on the jetty. We boarded the ferry boat next morning, and in an hour or so arrived at Gosaba, hungry, thirsty, dishevelled and dirty.

Gosaba was the brain-child of Sir Daniel Hamilton. In 1903, when middle-aged, he had made as much money as he wanted as a merchant. He had been a partner in the large firm of Mackinnan, Mackenzie & Co., of Calcutta. He had felt the need for something challenging, so he retired from his firm, and obtained a long lease from the government for the uninhabited island of Gosaba. He then collected a gang of down-and-outs and criminals from the slums of Calcutta and took them to Gosaba. With them he cleared the jungle, erected bunds (dried mud embankments), around the island to keep out the sea, sank artesian wells to obtain water for drinking and irrigation, dug up the soured soil and exposed it to the sunlight before growing rice. He then settled his gang of workers on the island, each receiving a loan of £20 for the purchase of agricultural tools. More down-and-outs arrived from Calcutta and the colony grew and prospered. He had to wage a constant war against a species of beetle that burrowed into the bunds, weakening them and threatening to breach them and so allow the sea to break through. The bunds needed to be patrolled and inspected daily. The colony had been in existence about thirty years when we visited it, yet daily patrols were still needed.

During those thirty years the island had prospered and had a population of 16,000. It was self supporting, managing its own affairs on a co-operative credit system. Rice of a high quality of selected seed was grown. Each village had its own Co-operative Society. There was a co-operative store for articles the villagers could not provide for themselves. There was a dispensary and a free health service provided from the profits of the co-operative societies. There were village primary schools, an English Middle School, a Weaving School and an Agricultural College, all provided from co-operative society funds. Sir Daniel was a Scot, he decided that education should be a strong feature of the island.

There was a large co-operative mill owned by 600 share-holders. The cultivators brought their grain to be husked at the mill, from where it was marketed by the Central Co-operative Paddy Sale Society in Calcutta. The island owned its own steamer. It even had its own currency. There was no police force and no crime, disputes were settled in the ancient Indian way by a Panchayat, a council of five village elders. Three groups of people had been banned from the island by Sir Daniel: money-lenders, lawyers and Roman Catholic Priests. Sir Daniel was a strict Presbyterian.

It had been a number of years since Sir Daniel had relinquished all control in the island; he was now in his seventies, but the island was managing its own affairs satisfactorily, and it was prospering. Sir Daniel visited the island for a month or two each year. The rest of the time he spent in Scotland where he had organised another agricultural colony on the same co-operative lines as at Gosaba.

We were fortunate in visiting the island when Sir Daniel was in residence. He entertained us and showed us round the island. During the evening he talked to us, teaching us the practical side of a co-operative movement. It was just what we were needing. This hard-headed business Scot impressed on us that enthusiasm, idealism and theories were not enough. For a co-operative society to succeed he emphasised that it must be founded on sound business lines. He told us that it would be necessary to be rather autocratic at the formation of a society, but that once it was on its feet we should withdraw. He gave us invaluable advice. The one evening made our long uncomfortable journey worthwhile; we returned to Itarsi much wiser.

Despite all the discomforts I rather enjoyed our 1,870 mile hippie jaunt. What I did not enjoy was the nasty attack of dysentry I went down with as soon as I got back, but I had rather asked for it.

We found that Jogneshwar Gogoi had arrived from Sevegram to join us when we got back from our long journey. Jug, as everyone called him, was a young man about 20 years old, from Assam. He had spent a year or two at Gandhi's ashram, learning village industries, spinning and weaving, and the construction of model village houses. He was a very lively person, with Mongolian features and a smiling face, was quite short, about five feet in height. It was amusing to see the diminutive Assamese with the tall German as they went about together. Jug was quite an acrobat, he could climb a tree like a monkey. He was a child of the Assam forests, but had shed the traditions and superstitions of his Hindu upbringing. He liked fun and had a delightful sense of humour.

While working in Itarsi he used to go back to Sevegram ashram for a day or two every now and then. On one occasion he went there when Lord Lothian was having discussions with Gandhi on behalf of the British Government. When Jug came back I asked him if he had seen Lord Lothian. "Yes", said Jug, "and he talked to me". "Did he", I said, "and what did he say to you?" Jug laughed and replied, "he said, 'please can you direct me to the latrines'".

After the war Jug came to England for a couple of years to study at a Co-operative College in Manchester. He spent some of the vacations with us in the Forest of Dean where I had settled. He told us that he had been attending Quaker Meetings in Manchester. When I asked him what he thought of them he grinned, saying that they were a good opportunity for him to practice public speaking. "Seriously, Jug", I said, "What do you think of them?" He thought for a while and then replied, "well, you sit and you sit and nobody says anything. Then you long for somebody to say something, and when somebody does speak you wish they would shut up." He went back to Assam from Manchester and eventually became quite a senior official in the Assam Government's Co-operatives.

Herbert and Jug quickly got down to work. The first co-operative producers' society they organised was for some weavers who lived in a small colony just outside the town, who were desperately poor and heavily in debt. With Herbert and Jug's encouragement and guidance they agreed to pool their resources and form a co-operative producers' society. In six months they were out of debt, and afterwards managed their own affairs with Herbert's guidance for a while. They did not become prosperous, but they were no longer poor or in debt.

The sanitation in the hospital troubled me a great deal. Also I disliked the employment of Sweepers, theirs seemed such a humiliating job, making them the lowest of the Untouchables. I heard of an American engineer who was doing rural reconstruction in another part of India. He had devised a very cheap septic tank suitable for a village house. In those days septic tanks were a new form of sanitation, they were not in general use as they are today. In England, at that time, one either had a flush toilet or an outside privy, there were no septic tanks.

I wrote to the American asking for information about their construction. He sent me the necessary details which were very simple. I then got together some unemployed lads from the town and taught them how to make septic tanks. I employed them to put septic tanks in all the hospital buildings that required them. I paid them a wage, but kept half of it back placing it in a central pool. When they had accumulated sufficient capital, I handed it and the lads over to Herbert and Jug, who organised them into a co-operative sanitation society.

It became very successful. Gandhi heard of it and was very interested in the scheme as it took away from the sweeper his degrading work. Jawarhalal Nehru visited us while the hospital work on septic tanks was in progress. He had not heard of septic tanks and insisted on going and having a look at them. In one of the ward's latrines we had a long conversation, lasting about half an hour, while I explained to him how they worked and how they were constructed. Nowadays I often wonder if there is anyone else who has had a half-hour's serious discussion with a Prime Minister in a Loo. Of course, it was some years later that he actually became Prime Minister. He later had septic tanks installed in his house in Allahabad.

Another project that Herbert and Jug started was a co-operative shop in the town. This was not quite so easy as a Producers' Society, we thought that there would be a lot of opposition from the merchants in the town. As it turned out the Co-op Shop met with very little antagonism. It was run by a Committee consisting of Herbert and Jug, a Hindu Gandhian Congress worker named Pagare, and a young Mohammedan school teacher who also fancied himself as something of a Poet. Pagares brother-in-law, Dongre, was appointed Manager. The shop became a great success.

We gave over a part of the hospital compound for Jug to build a small model village. When some of the houses were completed we tried to encourage the families of the patients in the wards to stay in them while their relatives were having treatment in the hospital. Jug explained to them how the model houses were constructed, complete with septic tanks, encouraging them to build one when they returned to their village. He also encouraged them to start spinning and weaving and other remunerative village industries. The model village became quite a social centre for the patients' relatives who otherwise had nothing to do, long discussions would take place with Jug about how the villagers could help themselves to raise their incomes and standard of living.

About a couple of months after Herbert started working at Itarsi a second Sister arrived at the hospital from England, Lucille Allen. She was half English and half Jamaican. She had had a good nursing training in England, and brought a new and refreshing atmosphere to the nursing staff. She made a great difference to the hospital, but did not always see eye to eye with the other Sister. That is putting it mildly! I welcomed the much needed changes she made. The day she arrived she met Herbert. They looked at each other, and that was that. Love at first sight. They were married a few weeks later.

Chapter Thirteen

Kamala Bhai

George Jones turned up unexpectedly. He had got himself tied up with Annie Besant's theosophy back in England, and decided that he must visit the land of its origin. He saved up the money for the fare, chucked up his job, and got on a boat for India. On arrival at Bombay he made straight for Itarsi, turning up out of the blue. Somebody back home had given him my name and address, I don't know who, or why, I was not involved in any way in the theosophy movement. He was engaged to a girl, Margaret, to whom theosophy made no appeal whatever.

After George had been with us a short while it gradually dawned on him that India was not quite like what he had imagined from reading his books on theosophy. He saw no contemplative orientals, no mystical mahatmas, no saintly sadhus in communication with the infinite. He saw suffering, disease, hunger, poverty, squalor. George put away his romanticisms and his fantasies, and accepted reality. He asked if he could help Herbert and Jug with their work, and his offer was warmly accepted. He became very happy doing practical things with them. He wrote and told his Margaret all about it. She replied, saying she would be coming out to join him as soon as she had worked out her notice to her employer; she had an office job in Southampton. She turned up a month or two later and there was another wedding. Margaret started working in the hospital. Although she had no nursing experience, Lucille took her under her wing and found plenty for her to do.

George was a hypersensitive person who became more and more obsessed with the poverty and suffering he saw around him. He became disturbed and sometimes almost irrational about it. At times we had to persuade him to eat his meals, he would think it wrong for him to eat when so many others were going hungry. Margaret was a person who always had her feet solidly on the ground. She tried to understand how he was feeling, and at the same time tried to help him to keep some sense of proportion. George would come back from a village distressed and depressed by the things he had seen. One day he went off and lived in a very poor Gond village about forty miles away. He lived with the Gonds, trying to share their life and eating the same sparse food as them. He would come back and see Margaret for a day or two every now and then. We all became very worried about him, as he got progressively thinner and weaker. Despite all our effortss to dissuade him from returning to the village he obstinately persisted in going back. Then one day we got a message to say that he had died. He had been doing manual work helping some Gonds to build houses. Apparently he had just lain down and died from weakness. We were very concerned now about Margaret, who was seven months pregnant. Shortly after George's death she went into premature labour and gave birth to a still-born baby.

When she had recovered from this we all assumed she would return to England. But we had under-estimated the strength and depth of Margaret's character. Instead of returning home she visited Gandhi and told him what had happened. She asked him what she could do to serve India in memory of George. Gandhi was very impressed by her personality but pointed out to her that she had no training of any sort. He said that India had use only for English people who had something practical to give, and sentimentality is unproductive. He suggested to her that she should go to the Wadia Maternity Hospital in Bombay where she could train as a Midwife. The training took two years, the other pupil Midwives with whom she would have to live were all Indians. This did not deter Margaret, she completed the two years training.

Gandhi never forget her. She would sometimes visit him when she had holidays from the training school. He said he regarded her as a daughter, gave her an Indian name, Kamala Bai. He wrote letters to her every now and then, some of that correspondence I have in my possession, it consists of just short notes, some on postcards.

After qualifying as a Midwife, Margaret worked in an Indian Village for a time. She then started a training school for Dhais at Gandhi's suggestion. Dhais are village midwives, who belong to the Sweeper caste, the lowest of the Untouchables. In India when a woman is in labour, and for two weeks afterwards, she is regarded as unclean. She is banished to an outhouse or cow shed for delivery, being attended to by a Dhai. At the end of the fortnight the woman performs certain religious purification rites and is then welcomed back into the family and the caste.

Midwifery in India is a dreadful affair. I have seen the most appalling cases. The Dhais are illiterate, ignorant, untrained, and with no regard for cleanliness. Their methods are of the crudest. At times they use cow dung as a lubricant. Deaths from neglected abnormal labour and from puerperal sepsis are only too common.

Margaret in her training school attempted to teach the Dhais simple hygiene and how to recognise the symptoms when things were going wrong. It was a thankless uphill fight against ignorance, stupidity, superstition and the conservatism of age-old customs. Some of the Dhais were sent to the training school against their wish from villages where Congress workers were trying to put Gandhi's ideas into practice. If Margaret persuaded one of them just to wash their hands in future during a delivery, that was a victory. It was a heart-breaking and seemingly hopeless task she had set herself. Only her patience, strength of character, and the support Gandhi gave her, kept her going.

Then, suddenly more urgent work called and challenged her. It was at the time of the partition of India. Up in the North there was savagery and slaughter and the flight of millions of refugees. Margaret set off to the stricken area to see what help she could give.

There, amid the violence, the murder, the rape, the looting and burning of buildings, she met up with another very brave woman, Lady Mountbatten. The Viceroy's wife had left the security and the comfort of the Viceregal Lodge in Delhi and had plunged into that violent and dangerous chaos to try to bring relief to the innocent victims. Without any thought for their own personal safety these two women organised emergency hospitals, enthusing helpers by their example. Their courage has gone unsung in the annals of history. No official honours were bestowed on Margaret. Some years later she developed cancer of the liver and returned to England in 1947. I looked after her in the Dilke Memorial Hospital until she died. She was one of the finest and most courageous women that I have known.

Chapter Fourteen
Fremlyn

The Reverend Fremlyn Streatfield was the garrison chaplain in Jubbulpore, which was 150 miles from Itarsi. He came once a month to give communion to a handful of C of E Eurasians who lived in Itarsi and were working for the GIP Railway. On his visits he used to stay at the Dak bungalow near the station. Dak bungalows were scattered all over India for Government Officials to stay in when on tour. They were dreary comfortless buildings with a minimum of furniture.

I first met Fremlyn one day as he was walking to the Dak bungalow from the Station, with his bearer carrying his bedding and his suitcase. He looked hot and tired in his linen clerical suit, he was sweating under his dog-collar.

"Why stay in that dreadful dismal place?" I said to him, "why not come and stay with us at the hospital when you visit Itarsi?" He did not know who I was, but anything must have seemed better than the loneliness and the cheerlessness of that Dak bungalow.

"That is very kind of you," he said. "You may find us a bit primitive compared with Jubbulpore", I told him, "but you will be very welcome". He came along with me to the hospital. I introduced him to the other members of our group. We were a mixed collection of Europeans and Indians, and must have seemed a rather strange unconventional, perhaps rather comic lot to him, compared with the garrison life in Jubbulpore. Later he dubbed us "The Itarsi Circus".

The next time he turned up to stay with us he was wearing shorts and an open shirt, his dog-collar was packed away with the bottle of communion wine.

He was always interested in meeting the various people who used to come and visit us. On one occasion he met Leonard Schiff, who had called to stay with us during his travels in India. He was engaged in writing a book about Indian politics and the independence movement. He was a flamboyant intellectual Jew in his late twenties, with a thick black beard. He wore Indian costume, and smoked a hookah. From his conversation it transpired that he posed as an admirer of Karl Marx.

He was soon in an animated discussion with Fremlyn, during the course of which Fremlyn said, "Of course, as a Journalist, you might not comprehend what I mean".

"I'm not a Journalist", said Schiff.

"What is your occupation?" asked Fremlyn.

"I am an Anglican priest", said Schiff.

Leonard Schiff later returned to England and was given a living some-where. Some years afterwards I met a chap who had lived in his parish for a time. He told me that Schiff had started his incumbency by having a big row with the parochial church council over a placard he had put up in the Church porch which read: "This Church was utterly restored in 1924". I don't know whether it is a true story, but I could believe it having met Schiff.

Fremlyn was middle-aged, had a pleasant round face, with blue eyes and thinning sandy-coloured hair. He was a sincere person who tried to prac-tice what he preached. He was not one of those all too common parsons who are socially pretentious and vocally artificial. I am sure that in the can-tonment in Jubbulpore he was as much loved as a friend as respected as the Chaplain. He had no pretentions, was incapable of talking with his tongue in his cheek.

In Jubbulpore the only Indians he met were clerks and servants, of the real Indians outside the cantonment he had no knowledge. One day I walked back with him to the Station to see him off back to Jubbulpore. He had spent the previous day with me on tour in the travelling dispensary, and had seen something of the real India he had not seen before, just a glimpse. He had seen the poverty in the villages and the wretched plight of the Gonds; he had seen misery he had not realised existed. It revealed a very different India from life in the cantonment. When the train drew into the Station, he got into a 3rd class compartment. I asked him why he was travelling 3rd class when he had a 1st class pass. He replied that he had swapped his pass for this journey for his bearer's 3rd class ticket.

I realised that what he had seen the day before had made him feel like the priest in the parable who had passed his stricken neighbour by on the other side, and he had been passing by for many years. Yesterday he had at least been like the Levite who had crossed the road and had a look. Fremlyn had now seen, but what could a garrison Chaplain do about it? Just nothing. But Fremlyn was a caring man, a man of compassion, he felt the need of some symbolic gesture to show he cared. This was what he was doing, identifying himself for a few brief hours with those at life's roadside stricken by pov-erty, exploitation, disease and despair.

I don't know who must have felt the more uncomfortable, Fremlyn sitting on the hard wooden seat the object of curiosity from forty pairs of eyes, or the bearer who did not feel at all at ease travelling like a Pukka Sahib in the air-conditioned 1st class compartment! I wondered what his C.O. back in Jubbulpore would say if he heard about it.

Fremlyn called us "The Itarsi Circus", not as a jibe, but as an affectionate nick-name. After the stifling conventions of the sahibs, and especially the memsahibs, in Jubbulpore, he loved being one of us for a short time. We were another world to him, just as the life style of the circus folk seems a strange sort of existence to us, entrapped as we are in our mass produced, pre-packaged rat-race society. I think he secretly envied us living in Itarsi.

When Fremlyn retired he settled down in Mitcheldean about ten miles from where I was living in the Forest of Dean, and we renewed our friendship. Alas, he is no more, and his church is the poorer for the loss of such as him.

Chapter Fifteen

Panditji

Jawaharlal Nehru kept his promise to visit Itarsi hospital. He turned up unexpectedly one day when he had to wait a few hours while changing trains on his way home to Allahabad. It was the first of a number of visits, some just for an hour or two, others for a few days. As a result of these visits the secret police started taking an active interest in our affairs. Although it annoyed us we did not let it bother us, we were not involved in politics, nothing we were doing could possibly have been regarded as subversive, quite the reverse. On one occasion a meeting was held in my bungalow between Nehru, an American named Edward C. Carter of the Institute of Pacific Relations, and Professors Pars Ram and S.K. Datta of Lahore. At this meeting arrangements were made for Nehru to go to China to meet Chiang Kai-shek, Carter was very anxious that the two should meet. Nehru later made the visit to China but I do not think he was very impressed by the Chinese Generalissimo. Anyhow, nothing materialised from the visit.

Nehru was a strange mixture of eastern and western cultures. East is east and west is west, and in Jawaharlal Nehru the twain did meet. He belonged to a wealthy Kashmiri family of brahminic origin. His father, Motilal Nehru, was a forceful and strong character, a very successful barrister who had settled in Allahabad. Born in 1889, Jawaharlal had a sheltered childhood, with private tutors until the age of 15 when he was sent to Harrow School in England. From Harrow he entered Trinity College, Cambridge. After graduation he studied law and in 1912 became a Barrister of the Inner Temple, and returned to India to practice law. He was a handsome man, with fine features and a sensitive face, like most Kashmiris he had a fair complexion and could easily have been mistaken for a European. He was not tall but had the body-build of an athlete.

A few years after his return to India from England two events occurred which were to change the course of his life. The first happened in 1919, he tells of it in his autobiography:

"Towards the end of that year I travelled from Amritsar to Delhi by the night train. The compartment I entered was almost full and all the berths, except one upper one, were occupied by sleeping passengers. I took the vacant upper berth. In the morning I discovered that all my fellow passengers were military officers. They conversed with each other in loud voices which I could not help over-hearing. One of them was holding forth in an aggressive and triumphant tone and soon I discovered that he was General

Dyer, the hero of Jallianwala Bagh, and he was describing his Amritsar experiences. He pointed out how he had the whole town at his mercy and he had felt like reducing the rebellious city to a heap of ashes, but he took pity on it and refrained. He was evidently coming back from Lahore after giving his evidence before the Hunter Committee of Inquiry. I was greatly shocked to hear his conversation and to observe his callous manner. He descended at Delhi Station in pyjamas with bright pink stripes and a dressing gown."

The second event occurred in June, 1920. He has written that at that time his political outlook was entirely bourgeois, and that he knew nothing of the conditions of the masses. One day a party of about two hundred Kisans (peasants) marched fifty miles from the interior to Allahabad in order to draw the attention of the local politicians to their condition. Almost out of curiousity Nehru went with some friends to the river bank where the party of Kisans had assembled. They told them of their plight, their poverty, their troubles and miseries, and of the inhuman treatment they received from the Landlords. They begged for a visit to the area so that the politicians could see for themselves what conditions were like. They were so persistent that in the end Nehru promised to visit them. A few days later, with some colleagues, he kept his promise, and the visit was a revelation to him. In his autobiography he writes as follows of the effect the visit had on him:

"They showered their affection on us and looked on us with loving and hopeful eyes, as if we were the bearers of good tidings, the guides who were to lead them to the promised land. Looking at them and their misery and over-flowing gratitude, I was filled with shame and sorrow, shame at my own easy going and comfortable life and our petty politics of the city which ignored this vast multitude of semi-naked sons and daughters of India, sorrow at the degradation and over-whelming poverty of India. A new picture of India seemed to rise before me, naked, starving, crushed and utterly miserable. And their faith in us, casual visitors from the distant city, embarrassed me and filled me with a new responsibility that frightened me.

I listed to their innumerable tales of sorrow, their crushing and ever-growing burden of rent, illegal exactions, ejectments from land and mud huts, beatingss; surrounded on all sides by vultures who preyed on them - Zamindars' agents; money-lenders; police; toiling all day to find that what they produced was not theirs and their reward was kicks and curses and a hungry stomach".

As a result of these and other incidents, Nehru eventually became involved with the Indian National Congress Party, and by doing so inevitably fell under the influence and spell of Gandhi. He soon became a leading figure in the Congress Party, being elected President in 1929, and was known throughout India as Panditji. He had a tremendous affection for Gandhi and great respect for his opinion. He constantly sought Gandhi's advice and became very close to him.

I got the impression, however, that for Nehru satiagraha was only a political weapon, the only weapon India had in her struggle for independence. Nehru was an agnostic, although he admitted that Buddhism had a strong attraction for him, while Gandhi was soaked in religion. Non-violence had no spiritual basis for Nehru. This is borne out by what Nehru wrote: "For us and for the National Congress as a whole the non-violent method was not, and could not be, a religion or an unchallengable creed or dogma. It could only be a policy and a method promising certain results, and by those results it would have to be finally judged. Individuals might make of it a religion or incontrovertible creed. But no political organisation, so long as it remained political, could do so".

When the Congress Party came to power, with Jawarharlal Nehru as the first Prime Minister, it virtually abandoned Gandhian principles. Although their first Act of Parliament was a Bill which made untouchability illegal, this was done as a gesture and tribute to Gandhi. By and large successive Congress Governments have been content to pay only lip-service to Gandhi and his ideals. The Untouchables are still being persecuted today, with even more violence than in Gandhi's time.

When Nehru made his visits to our hospital in Itarsi he appeared to enjoy them, and we certainly enjoyed having him. Sometimes when he came I had the feeling that he had had his fill of some of the petty squabbling inside the Congress Party. He sometimes seemed grateful to be away from it all for a time, and to be able to look at the problems of rural India away from political Party pressures.

He took a real interest in what we were trying to do, would discuss it with us, and would look at the problem of rural India with discerning eyes. I never discussed politics with him, except that one day I ventured to ask him what he would do with all the British people in India, the Civil Servants, Judges, District Commissioners, Army Officers, Forestry Officials, etc. if India should gain her independence the next day. He thought for a while, and then he quietly said, "I would put them all on a liner and send them away. Then, when the liner had about reached Aden, I would send them a wireless cable and invite them to come back". It was the way he put the emphasis on that word "invite" which was so revealing.

When the news leaked out that Nehru was at the hospital, crowds would gather at the entrance gate to await an opportunity to see him. As I drove him out of the compound to take him back to the station, a great cry of "Punditji Jawarharlal Nehru kijai" would burst out, to be repeated all the way to the station from the crowds of people who lined the roads, and he would smile and wave to them.

Nehru spent nine years of his life in jail. Two of the sentences were prolonged, during which he spent the time writing books, such as "The Discovery of India" and an Autobiography.

When he became India's first Prime Minister he strove to create a strong, centralised, industrialised, socialist nation state. This was the opposite from what Gandhi had envisaged after India had gained her freedom. Since over 90% of Indians lived in villages, Gandhi, in order to eliminate their poverty, wanted power to work upwards from the village periphery to a loose federation of states based on village republics. Under Nehru power was centralised. Industrialisation caused a drift from the poverty-stricken villages to the squalor of the over-populated cities, a drift which in recent years has reached alarming proportions. Nehru wanted India to be a democracy and he introduced adult suffrage. He could so easily have imposed his personal rule and become a dictator. He became involved in military actions he would rather have done without: the forcible seizure of the State of Hyderabad and of Portugese Goa; his quarrel with Pakistan over Kashmir; and the invasion by China which not only disillusioned him about his vision of China, but also revealed to him the inadequacies and inefficiencies of the Army's high command.

After independence there were many who jumped onto the Congress Party bandwaggon, wealthy landowners, industrialists and lawyers. They brought the evils of corruption with them, and corruption has grown and festered ever since. Those Gandhians who fought and suffered with Gandhi to gain India her freedom were not corrupt, Nehru was absolutely incorruptible. It was a weakness in him that being so honest and uncorrupt himself he was blind to corruption in others, although he could be testy and short tempered at times. He was too decent a man to be ruthless when ruthlessness was necessary to combat corruption and inefficiency. That was his weakness as a Politician - his innate sensitivity and decency. Unfortunately, but realistically, there seems to be little room for decency in politics.

Jawarharlal Nehru was not only India's first Prime Minister, he was also a world statesman. In the field of foreign policy he was the creator of non-alignment, keeping India completely independent of the two larger power blocs, a policy afterwards adopted by many newly independent countries to form a sort of club of non-aligned states that persists today. He also kept India within the British Commonwealth.

Jawarharlal Nehru was Prime Minister of India for seventeen years. He died on May 27th, 1964, and passed into history.

Chapter Sixteen

The Walking Saint

After his assassination Gandhi's spiritual mantle descended on Acharya Vinoba Bhave. In the early days of the Sabarmati ashram, Gandhi had recognised the sincerity and depth of Vinoba's spirituality, and had chosen him to be the first of his followers to be trained as a Satyagrahi. He was now a frail, elderly man; lean, tall, straight, with a flowing white beard. His health was poor and he suffered much pain from a gastric ulcer. Now that Gandhi was dead he was concerned to keep alive the emphasis on the poverty of the villages and the spiritual basis of Gandhi's teaching.
. Sevagram Ashram continued after Gandhi's death but it was not the same, Congress leaders no longer visited it, they were too busy at the seat of government. Some Gandhian workers who had no personal political ambitions endeavoured to keep the ashram alive, to maintain the atmosphere Gandhi had created. They continued working there, but were ignored by the Congress Government. Many of the landlord class had now joined the Congress Party and were a powerful political lobby. Vinoba wanted them to relinquish some of their land and distribute it voluntarily to landless peasants. In China Mao Tse-tung and his revolutionaries had ruthlessly slaughtered the entire landlord class which had stood in the way of land reform, but this was not Gandhi's or Vinoba's way.

Vinoba decided to try persuasion. He started the Bhoodan movement, and marched on foot with a band of Gandhian followers across the length and breadth of India visiting as many villages as he could. He endeavoured to persuade the landowners in the villagers to part with some of their land so that it could be divided up and distributed to landless peasants. He quoted the Hindu scriptures and appealed to their consciences and their better nature. The Bhoodan movement aroused a considerable degree of popular support, Vinoba Bhave had long been revered as a Saint by the Indian people. All over India and beyond the news of the "Saint on the March" spread. He attracted many who marched with him. The landowners found it difficult to resist Vinoba's gentle persuasion backed up as it was by so much public moral pressure; some of them sincerely responded to Vinoba's appeal, others just wanted to save face. When Vinoba had been successful in a village, a Gandhian worker who had been one of the marchers would remain behind to help and advise on the re-distribution of the land and would encourage co-operative ventures.

When Mrs Indira Gandhi, the Indian Prime Minister, declared the State of Emergency in June 1975, and assumed dictatorial powers, Vinoba was

81 years old. Protest at Mrs Gandhi's action came from all over India and beyond. Non-violent Gandhian workers were imprisoned without trial, and many of them tortured. Vinoba was still a much respected figure. He offered satyagraha as a protest, and decided to go on a fast. He demanded a complete ban on cow slaughter by the Government throughout India. This had a symbolic importance for millions of Indians for whom the cow is a sacred animal. Just as Gandhi had used the Salt Laws as a weapon against the British Raj, so Vinoba used cow slaughter against the Indian Dictatorship. He declared that agriculture is the backbone of the Indian economy and that the cow is essential for agriculture. The Indian Constitution has stated that the cow must be protected, but the Government had not implemented this, thousands of cows were being slaughtered. Vinoba's ashram was raided by the police, who seized all the copies of his monthly journal. After the raid Vinoba suspended publication of further numbers of the journal. He stated, "What cowards we have become that the newspapers have not published the news of my fast because the Government has censored it. If I were to die because of this fast, and the Government propagated that death was due to heart failure, then would all the newspapers publish this governmental version."

Vinoba had earlier attracted to the Bhoodam movement a Socialist Politician, a Gandhian, Jayaprakash Narayan, who was until then considered to be Nehru's natural successor as Prime Minister. Jayaprakash had become disgusted with the corruption in Indian politics and abandoned it, devoting all his activities to Vinoba's Bhoodan movement.

The landlord class has had its chance to avoid the possibility in the future of having their land wrested from them by violence. For the most part they are a greedy set of men, unmoved by the suffering of the peasants. This is one of the many factors that lie at the heart of India's suffering, as in other parts of the world. As Mother Teresa of Calcutta has said, "The greatest evil today is the lack of love and charity, the terrible indifference towards one's neighbour who lies at the roadside assaulted by exploitation, corruption, poverty and disease."

In 1960, Nehru, addressing the Federation of Indian Chambers of Commerce stated, "I dislike the vulgarity of the rich as much as the poverty of the poor." Mahatma Gandhi went more to the heart of the matter when he said, "God gives enough for each man's need but not enough for each man's greed."

This latter was the basis of the philosophy of Narayan and Acharya Vinoba Bhave.

Chapter Seventeen

J.P.

Jayaprakash Narayan died in October, 1979, at the age of 76. He was known throughout India simply as J.P.

I first met him at Sevagram ashram and took an instant liking to him. He visited us at Itarsi on numerous occasions. He was born in a village in Bihar, went to the village school and won a scholarship to Patna University. In 1922 he went to America and attended Iowa State University, paying his way by working in the Chicago stockyards. He stayed in America for seven years.

When he returned to India he was a fiery nationalist and socialist, ready to fight British Imperialism by resorting to violence. He eventually became attracted to Gandhi who called him his problem child. Gradually, under Gandhi's influence, he renounced violence and embraced satyagraha. He became devoted to Gandhi, and joined the Indian Congress Party.

After independence, in 1957, he withdrew from politics, disillusioned with the Congress Party, and joined Vinoba's Bhoodan movement.

He had until then been regarded as Nehru's successor as Prime Minister. In the summer of 1958 he visited England with his wife. He stayed with us for a few days in the Forest of Dean, and spoke at a U.N. meeting in Coleford which was well attended. The following is the report of the meeting in the Dean Forest Journal of July 4th, 1958.

Dean Forest Guardian
Friday, July 4, 1958

Extending the Belief in Non-Violence

"A distinguished visitor from India, Mr Jayaprakash Narayan, once spoken of as Mr Nehru's probable successor, but who has left politics to associate himself with the policy of Vinoba Bhave, was the Speaker at a well attended meeting in the Council Chamber, Coleford, organised by the Coleford Branch of the United Nations Association, on Monday.

Mr Narayan described Vinoba Bhave as a "brilliant linguist", a deeply religious person, who had renounced the world, who looked towards spiritual rather than economic ends and who had started a movement which might be described as an extension of the work which Gandhi was doing, and which was interrupted by his assassination. He told how Vinoba went to a district where Communism was rife to preach non-violence and was challenged by an old landless Untouchable who spoke of his need for land. Vinoba appealed for land for this and other landless peasants, and a landowner at his meeting offered 100 acres. So started the movement that in a few years has resulted in voluntary gifts of more than 4,500,000 acres of land.

That represented the earliest phase of the movement, a voluntary relinquishment by landowners of part of their estates, but a later development has been the voluntary cession of all landed property and in 4,000 villages in India the whole of the land has become communal property. They hoped eventually to extend the movement to all the 500,000 villages in India. This concept of sharing might become universal and extended to industry to found a new industrial organisation.

Vinoba Bhave believed that India should unilaterally adopt a policy of disarmament and his movement aims to prepare people's minds for that possibility. As they had fought for their freedom without arms, could they not also defend it without arms?

Soldiers of Peace

Vinoba had called for 75,000 volunteers to be Soldiers of Peace. These, of whom he and wife were two, would be engaged in full-time service for a community of 5,000 people each and would be maintained by the community. These volunteers could not belong to any political party, should not believe in caste differences and should treat all religions as equal.

Vinoba's was a philosophy of love and truth, and realised as Mahatma Gandhi had done that changing social institutions would not mean much unless man himself changes.

The Rev. J.R. Mountney proposed a vote of thanks which was seconded by Mr M.G. Dawbarn. A member of the branch, Mr T. Bright, acted as Chairman."

In 1974, appalled at the extent of corruption during Mrs Indira Gandhi's Premiership, he returned to public life. He spoke out loudly and fearlessly against the corruption in the government and the machinations of the black markets in food. India was having to import enormous quantities of grain. J.P. wrote: "Those who think that sarvodaya is made up of goody-goody people, who no doubt talk of non-violent revolution but do not mean it seriously are in for a surprise. Speaking for myself I cannot remain a silent spectator to misgovernment, corruption and the rest, whether in Patna, Delhi, or elsewhere. It is not for this that I at least had fought for freedom. I am not interested in this or that Ministry being replaced or the Assembly being dissolved. These are partisan aims and their achievement will make no difference. It will be like replacing Tweedledum for Tweedledee. But I have decided to fight corruption and mis-government and black-marketing, profiteering and hoarding, to fight for the overhaul of the educational system, and for a real people's democracy."

In June 1975 Mrs. Indira Gandhi, the Prime Minister (Nehru's daughter, the widow of a Parsee lawyer and no relation to the Mahatma), suddenly announced a State of Emergency and dictatorial powers. She had been found guilty in a Court of Law of corrupt electoral practices. She imprisoned the entire parliamentary opposition and many others, including Jayaprakash Narayan. What she had to fear from this elderly widower now suffering from a kidney disease one cannot understand, unless it was the truth. Mrs Gandhi's restrictions included press censorship, the right of assembly, police powers of arrest and detention without trial. She arranged for the law to be altered retrospectively so that she could be found not guilty of corrupt electoral practices by an Appeal Court. She arrested a considerable number of judges and lawyers who resisted her decrees, especially those concerned with civil liberties.

There was arbitrary eviction of many thousands of house-owners and shopkeepers. Their premises were demolished with bulldozers, and the sites sold to commercial bidders. The evicted inhabitants were re-settled elsewhere in colonies in mosquito infested swamps where they lived a sub-human existence without adequate shelter, sanitation or water. Mrs Gandhi was much under the influence of her son, the notorious Sanjay, who initiated a sterilisation campaign as a method of compulsory birth-control. At its peak the campaign resorted to with-holding Government salaries, licenses, and essential services unless arbitrarily imposed sterilisation quotas were met. The campaign also involved the frequent use of the police for the forcible seizure of random groups and individuals for sterilisation.

After six months she released Jayaprakash from prison because of his failing health. While in jail he had written her a letter dated July 1st, 1975, smuggling a copy of it out of prison. The letter was circulated secretly in India among opponents of the State of Emergency. A copy was obtained by a Sunday Times Journalist; the newspaper published the letter in February 1976. It reads:

"You know I am an old man. My life's work is done, and after Prabha's (his wife) going I have nothing and no-one to live for...I have given all my life, after finishing education, to the country and ask for nothing in return. So, I shall be content to die a prisoner under your regime.

Would you listen to the advice of such a man? Please do not destroy the foundations that the Father of the Nation, including your noble father, laid down. There is nothing but strife and suffering along the path you have taken. You inherited a great tradition, noble values, and a working democracy. Do not leave behind a miserable wreck of all that.

It would take a long time to put all that together again. For it would be put together again, I have no doubt. A people who fought British Imperialism and humbled it, cannot accept indefinitely the indignity and shame of totalitarianism. The spirit of man can never be vanquished, no matter how deeply suppressed. In establishing your personal dictatorship you have buried it deep. But it will rise from the grave. Even in Russia it is slowly coming up.

You have talked of social democracy. What a beautiful image those words call to the mind. But you have seen in Eastern and Central Europe how ugly is the reality. Naked dictatorship and in the ultimate analysis Russian over-lordship. Please, please do not push India towards that terrible fate.

And may I ask to what purpose all these draconian measures? In order to be able to carry out your 20 points? But who was preventing you from carrying out the points? All the discontent, the protest, the satyagraha due precisely to the fact that you were not doing anything to implement your programme, inadequate as it was, to lighten the burden under which the people and the youth were groaning. This is what Chandra Shekhai, Mohan Dharis, Krishan Kant and their friends have been saying for which they have been punished. You have talked of "drift" in the country. But was that due to the opposition or to me? The drift was because of your lack of decision, direction and drive. You seem to act swiftly and dramatically only when your personal position is threatened. Once that is assured, the drift begins. Dear Indiraji, please do not identify yourself with the nation. You are not immortal, India is.

You have accused the opposition and me of every kind of villainy. But let me assure you that if you do the right things, for instance, your 20 points, tackling corruption at Ministerial levels, electoral reforms, etc, take the Opposition into confidence, heed its advice, you will receive the willing co-operation of every one of us. For that you need not destroy democracy. The ball is in your court. It is for you to decide. With these parting words, let me bid you farewell. May God be with you."

After release from prison Jayaprakash Narayan was put under home arrest, living in a shabby flat in Bombay. He was an invalid with failing kidneys, spending every second day locked into a dialysis machine. Even so he continued as an outspoken critic of Mrs Gandhi. Much of his criticism was suppressed however, because of the strict censorship of the Press.

In March 1977 Mrs Gandhi called a general election. She was so much out of touch with the people that she expected to be returned to power, but the Indian people had had enough. There was a groundswell of discontent. Mrs Gandhi's aunt, Jawarharlal's sister, Mrs Vijayalakshmi Pandit, now aged 76, emerged from her retirement and campaigned against her niece. She had retired in 1970 to live in Dehra Dun in the foothills of the Himalayas, having held her brother's Parliamentary Seat after his death. Prior to sitting in Parliament, she had been Ambassador in Moscow, and High Commissioner in London. In Parliament, she said, there was too much corruption and too little power. She disliked her nephew, Sanjay, calling him a rude, crude young man. Mrs Pandit was a beautiful, charming and cultured woman.

At the election Mrs Gandhi and the Congress Party were swept from power. J.P. was consulted by the various political parties and he advised that all the opposition parties should unite as the Janata Party under

Morarji Desai's Premiership. But he had only exchanged Tweedledee for Tweedledum.

J.P. was held in so much affection in India that in the Autumn of 1977 there was a countrywide collection for his 75th birthday. 7½ million rupees was the target (500,000 pounds), it was over-subscribed, 9 million rupees were collected. J.P. used the money to promote non-party grass roots people's committees as an effort to introduce social change.

Corruption persisted in the Janata Party. The various parties of which it consisted bickered and quarrelled amongst themselves instead of tackling India's problems. J.P. was approached to patch things up between the warring factions and heal the breeches. But J.P. was bitterly disillusioned with the Janata Party, he refused to help, he had had enough.

In 1979 a General Election was called. The Janata Party was annihilated and Mrs Gandhi was swept to power in a landslide victory. The people seemed to have forgotten what had happened under her State of Emergency. She was Prime Minister again.

Mrs Gandhi ruled a nation of over 314 million people, most of them poverty stricken. Her eldest son, Sanjay, whom was being groomed to succeed her was killed piloting his private plane. His brother, Rajiv, is being groomed to take his place and to found and perpetuate a Nehru dynasty, which is the last thing that Jawarharlal Nehru, a devoted democrat, would have wanted, as J.P. well knew. Jawarharlal did not groom his daughter to succeed him.

In October 1984 Indira Gandhi was assassinated.

Chapter Eighteen

Some More Gandhians

One of the most delightful characters I met was Saroniji Naidu. She was often at Sevagram. The first Indian woman to obtain a Cambridge degree, she blossomed out as a Poetess in the early years of this century. She wrote poems of distinction in the English language. Edmund Gosse wrote that "she must be given a page in any book of English Literature". In 1914 she met Gandhi and joined the national struggle for independence. She then stopped writing English poetry. She had indomitable courage and vision. She repeatedly illegally picketed government liquor shops, and served a number of prison sentences. In 1925 she was elected President of the Congress Party.

When I met her at Sevagram she was not all what I had imagined an Indian Poetess would look like. She was a dark, plump, dumpy, middle-aged woman with a round face, thick lips and a coarse skin. Her face was usually smiling; a vivid personality, Nehru once described her as a "pillar of fire". She was full of fun, loved teasing Gandhi, and once asked him if he realised how much it cost to keep him poor. She called him Mickey Mouse. She had a particularly unique influence on the nationalist struggle and the Congress Party, because she endeavoured to keep alive within it the rich cultural heritage of India, in which she herself was steeped. She was also an international figure, interpreting Indian culture to the West.

She was in Delhi at the time of Gandhi's murder, and hurried round to the compound where Gandhi's body lay as soon as she heard the news. She looked at the women weeping and sobbing as they sat around the blood-stained corpse. "What is all this snivelling about?" she exclaimed. "Would you rather he died of old age or indigestion? This is the only death great enough for him." After independence Saroniji Naidu was appointed Governor of Uttar Pradesh, the most heavily populated state in India. She died in office in 1949.

Gandhi's Secretary, Mahadev Desai, was the son of a village school teacher who grew up in a poor home. He became a translator and then a lawyer. Unable to make much money as a lawyer he got a job as a bank-inspector of farming co-operatives. This involved him in visiting the villages around Ahmedabad. He loved villages, village life and village people and learnt the various dialects and collected their songs. When he was twenty-five years old, he met Gandhi who was then twice his age. Gandhi took an instant liking to him, saying he had found in him his "perfect son".

Mahadev Desai served Gandhi faithfully and loyally for the remainder of his life. He also edited Gandhi's weekly newspaper, "The Harijan". He was a gentle person with a nice sense of humour. The first time I met him he was enjoying a good laugh as he was typing an article of Gandhi's for the next issue of "The Harijan". It was an article condemning the use of all machines. Gandhi had handed the article to him and asked him to type it out. "Isn't a typewriter a machine?" Mahadev asked me, laughing.

Gandhi had another Secretary, an English woman, Madeleine Slade. She was the daughter of a British Admiral. A tall, handsome young woman, she had received an excellent education. By chance she read a book, Romain Rolland's "Life of Gandhi". The book so appealed to her that she decided she must join Gandhi's ashram. She spent a whole year preparing herself. She learnt spinning, became a vegetarian, slept on the floor, and studied the Hindu scriptures. In 1925 she left England for India and joined Gandhi's ashram.

Gandhi welcomed her, called her his daughter, and gave her an Indian name, Mira Ben. It created quite a stir in the British press, which vilified her, smearing her with most unpleasant innuendos of a sexual nature, all of which were false. It was a campaign, politically motivated, to discredit Gandhi. Madeleine Slade, or Mira Ben as she now became, was a deeply religious woman. Her decision to join Gandhi in his work was akin to that of a young woman with a vocation to become a Nun.

I found her to be a very serious woman, distant and somewhat withdrawn. She was a very efficient Secretary, serving Gandhi until his death, after which she retired to Switzerland.

She returned to England for a short visit in 1969 for the celebrations during Gandhi's centenary year. She received great applause when she appeared at the Albert Hall together with other celebrities, including Lord Louis Mountbatten. She was then a tall, frail, dignified old lady.

This occasion had been preceded by a Centenary Memorial Service in St. Paul's Cathedral which was televised and recorded. It commenced and ended with the singing to Indian instruments of Hindu hymns by a group of Indian singers led by the celebrated singer Surya Kumari. It was the first time that non-Christian, as well as Christian, hymns had been sung in the Cathedral. The Christian hymns were "Lead Kindly Light" and "When I Survey the Wondrous Cross", two favourites of Gandhi. The Addresses were given by the Archbishop of Canterbury and Lord Louis Mountbatten. The service concluded with a recording of Gandhi's voice speaking in English. It was a unique tribute to somebody, a Hindu, who had toppled our empire. I have a recording of the service.

Gandhi was concerned to do something about the problem of illiteracy. He instituted in the village school in Savagram a system which he called Basic Education, which he wished to be adopted in all the villages in India. He did not agree with the educational system instituted under the British Raj which was modelled on the English type and had no relation to Indian village life. He put this work for Basic Education into the hands of Aryanakham and his wife.

They were a charming couple with whom I became very friendly. Aryanakham was a tall, very handsome man who held a degree from a British University. Born a Christian he had been baptised with the name Aryan Williams. Returning to India after obtaining his British degree he joined the Independence Movement and changed his name to Aryanakham. His wife, Asha Devi, was a Brahmin, with a Ph.D., from Calcutta University. It was most unusual for a Christian to marry a Brahmin. She remained a Hindu throughout her marriage. They had two children. Tragedy came to them when one of the children, a boy, was accidentally poisoned when he helped himself to a bottleful of sugar-coated quinine tablets. They were frequent visitors to Itarsi.

Later, Aryanakham paid two visitss to England. He stayed with me in the Forest of Dean on both occasions. On his second visit he looked far from well, and I discovered that he had a severe degree of diabetes. He died in India a few years later.

Gandhi's ideas on Basic Education were first put into practice by the Aryanakhams in the village school in Sevagram. Later they were put in charge of a Teachers' Training School at Sevagram where young men and women from all over India came to be trained in basic education methods. These were profoundly different from those of the official ones which were Western orientated.

The children were put to work in miniature farms, the curriculum being related to the work they did, and would do when they grew up. Gandhi hoped that when the National Congress came to power it would make it the official type of education for all the villages in India, but it was not to be. The Aryanakhams remained at Sevagram after Gandhi's death, persevering with basic education hoping that the Congress government would change its mind, but the politicians were not interested. This gifted and devoted pair had sadness and disappointment at the end of their lives, seeing all that they had lived and worked for ignored by the Congress Party they had so wholeheartedly supported. It is interesting, however, that President Julius Nyerere has introduced1 Gandhi's ideas of Basic Education, and made it official, for Tanzania, with encouraging results.

The most imposing personality I met at Sevagram was Sardar Vallabhbhai Patel. He was then middle-aged tall and thick set, impressive in manner, appearing rather unapproachable on first acquaintance, which hid a warm-heartedness.

He first met Gandhi in 1917 in Kaira where he practised as a Lawyer. He was then rich, well-dressed, fond of whisky and cigars and the good things of life, very much a man of the world. He was a very able Lawyer. In 1917 there was trouble in Kaira district when the crops failed. The peasants were tenants of the Government, and usually when the crops failed the Government reduced the amount of the tax on the land. In 1917 it refused to admit that there was a crop failure. The peasants were unable to pay the full tax. Sardar Patel was acting for the tenants to present their case. He had heard of Gandhi and his reputation as a champion of the poor and that he was a Barrister.

He sent for Gandhi, and together they toured the district, collecting information from village to village to find out the extent of the crop failure in order to have the facts with which to petition the Government and request the usual reduction of tax.

They were an odd pair as they journeyed on their fact-finding tour. The tall, well-dressed, stoutish worldly man, accompanied by the small, thin, half-naked individual in a peasant's dhoti. Such was the effect of the little man on the big man that on their return, Sardar Patel threw up his practice, gave up whisky, cigars, his European clothes, and championing Gandhi, devoted the remainder of his life to the cause of India's peasantry.

He joined the National Congress in its struggle for independence. He became renowned as a great organiser and leader of the masses, and was absolutely loyal to Gandhi. Twenty years after his journey with Gandhi, he made a speech in Ahmedabad in which he said, "True socialism lies in the development of village industries. We do not want to reproduce in our country the chaotic conditions prevalent in the Western countries consequent on mass-production". Words which have been ignored.

When the first Congress Government was formed he was appointed Home Minister. One of his tasks was to weld and integrate the five hundred or more princely states, some large, some small, all in different stages of autocracy and feudalism, into the Union of India in a peaceful manner. In this, with the one exception of Hyderabad state, he succeeded.

At the start of Nehru's premiership, he quarrelled with him, possibly because he envied Nehru's position, but more likely because of Nehru's more westernised approach and his emphasis on industrialisation. On the morning of Gandhi's assassination Gandhi had sent for Sardar Patel. They had a long conversation during which Gandhi persuaded him to promise that he would stop quarrelling with Nehru and help him to govern India. Sardar Patel promised and kept that promise for the remainder of his life. Sardar Patel died in 1949, mourned by the entire nation.

Rajendra Prasad was a very different personality from Sardar Vallabhbhai Patel. Rajendra was an introvert, Sardar Patel an extrovert. When I first visited Sevagram Rajendra Prasad had recently returned from doing a magnificent job of organising relief work after the Behar earthquake, Behar being his province. Of peasant stock he was nevertheless a wealthy lawyer, until he gave up his lucrative practice at the Bar to join Gandhi. Nehru wrote of him, "his outstanding ability, his perfect straightness, his energy, and his devotion to the cause of Indian freedom are qualities which have made him loved not only in his own province but throughout India. Few others, if any, can be said to have imbibed more thoroughly the real message of Gandhi."

When I met him I thought him to be a shy, rather tense man. In 1946 an Indian Constitutional Assembly was created to frame a constitution for India, Rajendra Prasad being elected President. In 1950 he became the first President of the Republic of India.

Mary Barr, an English woman, was another Gandhian I knew. As a young woman she had gone to South Africa to visit her father who was living there. This was round about 1912. The South African government had just passed a new law according to which only Christian marriages, or marriages by an official Registrar, were legal. This upset the large Indian community, much of which was indentured labour.

Both Hindus and Moslems had always been married by their own priests. By the passing of this new Act their marriages were not recognised which made their children illegitimate. Gandhi, who was then living in South Africa practising as a lawyer, protested to General Smuts, the Prime Minister, but to no avail. Some Indian women who revered Gandhi and his satiagraha teaching took non-violent action. To enter South Africa required a permit. This group of Indian women, in order to demonstrate publicly, but non-violently, against the iniquity of the new Act, smuggled themselves out of the country one night. Next morning they crossed back across the border without their permits. They were arrested and sent to jail with their babies. There was an outcry in the world press about this action of the South African government.

The young Mary Barr was shocked and protested publicly for which she herself was arrested and sent to prison for six months. In prison she met the group of Indian women, got to know them, and made friends with them. The Act was eventually repealed by the government in the face of world reaction and protests from Whitehall. The then Viceroy of India made a famous speech siding with the group of Indian women and praising Gandhi and his non-violence.

On discharge from prison Mary Barr went to India and devoted the rest of her life to it. She stayed in Gandhi's ashram for a time, learned spinning and weaving, the Hindi language and Indian customs. Then she went to live in a large village, about forty miles from Itarsi. She lived, ate, cooked and dressed like the ordinary village folk. She taught them spinning and weaving, visited and tended their sick, encouraged and helped them in their troubles, told them about Gandhi and what he was doing to help village life. She became a friend to everybody in that village.

She was a Quaker, but she kept herself quite independent of the Quaker establishment. She lived very simply on a little pocket-money provided from Gandhi's ashram funds. She had been living in the village a number of years when I first got to know her. She went on living there until she was too old to look after herself. She was then taken by some friends to live in the Nilgri Hills in South India where she could be taken care of, and there she died.

I got to know her quite well. She was a small, quiet, rather demure woman, nothing ruffled her. She had great strength of character in a subdued kind of way. In her opinion imperialism was morally wrong, but she was not the sort of person to return to England and agitate against it, to protest in marches, to wave banners, to join an anti-imperialist league, she believed that got nobody anywhere. She was not an "anti" she was a "pro". She just stayed in that Indian village, loving the people living in it, being their friend and helping them. Her's was not a protest it was an example. To spend her whole life doing just that showed her sincerity and inner strength. She was a very remarkable person.

Another interesting character was C F Andrews. As a young man he had been ordained an Anglican priest, but later dissociated himself from the Anglican establishment and the Church Missionary Society, regarding them as tools of British imperialism. He became a free-lance priest, spending his time divided between England and India. In England he was concerned to awaken the Christian conscience regarding India, talking, lecturing and writing books and pamphlets. He wrote a widely read book: "The Christ of the Indian Road." In India he travelled extensively making friends with all sorts of people, including the Congress leaders and workers.

He became very close to Gandhi, who regarded him as one of his closest friends. Whenever Gandhi undertook a fast, or at any time of crisis, C F Andrews would be at his side, sometimes travelling long distances to be there. He would sit with him, listen to him, talk to him and reason with him, Gandhi relied very much on his presence and his friendship. C F Andrews was revered throughout India by everybody, British and Indian alike.

He came to stay at Itarsi hospital for a short time. He was then elderly, a tall thin man with a ruddy face and a long flowing white beard. He looked rather like the traditional Father Christmas. He died not long after his visit to the hospital. I can remember quite clearly the last I saw of him. I had gone to the station with him to see him off on the train. He had been leaning out of the window chatting to me, when, just as the train started to move off, he suddenly reached for his hold-all, opened it and started rummaging amongst its content. As the train gathered speed he threw something out of the window, shouting, "I've no use for this, it is too uncomfortable. Give it to one of your patients." As the train disappeared from the station I walked along the platform to pick up what he had thrown out. It was a truss. It seems a strange last memory to have of C F Andrews.

Nehru, in his Autobiography, wrote of him, "India does not possess a more devoted friend than Charlie Andrews, whose abounding love and spirit of service and over-flowing friendliness it is a joy to have." Gandhi said that the initials C.F.A. stood not only for Charles F. Andrews but also for Christ's Faithful Apostle.

I have written about Gandhi, and the Gandhians whom I met in the 1930's before India gained her freedom from Imperialism. If they could see their Mother India today, after over thirty years of independence, they would break their hearts. She is not the India they had envisaged and for which they had sacrificed their careers, had worked for, suffered for, served prison sentences for. India is now free from British domination, and the manner in which the transfer of power was effected is something Britain can be proud of, she left no legacy of bitterness or hatred behind her.

But India is not free, she is in the grip of greedy and corrupt politicians, landlords and industrialists. As Gandhi said, India will only be free when its villages are free from poverty. There are too many westernised Indians who admire and emulate the Western way of life and its technology, who have thrown away their country's rich cultural heritage. They seek only money, and despise and could not care less for the poverty stricken masses in the villages and towns. India is a land of ostentatious wealth side by side with the most abject poverty.

The Gandhian revolution was unique in history, to have been an observer from the inside was a fascinating experience. The personalities involved were inspired, dedicated and free from hatred, consumed with love for their country and the longing to see her free. Even after forty or more years the memory of them is still fresh.

But their Mother India today is not what they had envisaged. India today has an illiterate population of over 314 million. It has many universities, the largest number of scientists outside the USA and the USSR. It has a large army and airforce, can launch a satellite or explode a nuclear device, can build aircraft and ships. But it cannot bring prosperity, education or even enough food for the vast majority of its people, aims which were Gandhi's. The plight of the millions of untouchables, Gandhi's "children of God", is as bad as when Gandhi was alive. India with its glaring discrepancy between a few opulent rich and millions of poverty stricken peasants and pavement dwellers in its cities could not have been worse off if she had adopted what Gandhi advocated, power from the grass roots in a village democracy growing upwards, instead of centralised power. Indeed, she could have been much better off.

There are a few caring and devoted young Indian men and women who are devoting their lives to uplifting the villages by such measures as co-operatives with success, but they are few and far between and the villages are many. They are the true successors to the Gandhian revolution.

Chapter Nineteen

The Old Sausage Doctor

When I had been in India for a year or two it became necessary for me to return to England for a very brief visit. It was soon after Italy had invaded Abyssinia. I stayed with my brother-in-law and his wife in their small cottage in an Essex village.

In the evening my brother-in-law took me for a visit to his local, where, ensconced in his reserved corner, was the village doctor who had been in practice in the village for many years and was still practising. He had recently celebrated his ninetieth birthday, and gossip had it that he was living in sin with the retired village midwife. I don't expect he made much of a living in his practice, but he was part owner of a sausage factory in the village which provided him with a modest income. The sausages were something special, and famous in the district. Apart from his income from the sausage factory he had now simplified his personal finances - he sent no bills to his patients and he paid no bills to anyone.

My brother-in-law introduced me to him and we sat down and joined him in his corner. A middle-aged man came up to the doctor and reminded him that he had not yet paid the £40 for the Morris car he had sold him sometime ago. The old man stood up to his full height, his thick eye-brows bristled, he went red in the face. "So you are waiting for your money, are you"? he said, "how dare you approach me about it. You are complaining that you are being kept waiting for your money, are you? Well let me tell you something. I am still waiting for my fee from your Mother which she owes me for bringing you into the world. And you think you are being kept waiting!"

My brother-in-law bought the old man a drink to calm him down and mentioned that I worked in India, and was over for a brief visit. "India, is it", said the old doctor, "you can thank your lucky stars it isn't Abyssinia. There's a war going on there, a nasty one. I wouldn't like to be an Italian soldier captured by the Abyssinians. They are a savage uncivilised lot. Do you know what they do to their prisoners? They castrate them."

When I finally left India for good some years later, prior to my settling in the Forest of Dean, I paid my brother-in-law a visit. We popped down to the local as before. The old doctor was still there, settled down in his corner, so we went over to him. My brother-in-law asked him if he remembered me. "Remember him?", said the old doctor, "of course I remember him". Then turning to me, in a loud voice in that crowded bar he announced "You are the young fellow that got castrated in Abyssinia, aren't you?"

Chapter Twenty
Over the Bridge

After I left India I took over a practice in the Forest of Dean. Leaving the family to follow a few weeks later, I motored down from Birmingham travelling through Worcester, Malvern, Ledbury to Ross-on-Wye, then along the Herefordshire side of the River Wye to Goodrich, and crossed to the Gloucestershire side of the river over Huntsham Bridge. I remember that day and how very green England looked after the brown parched earth of India. Stopping the car on the bridge I got out and looked down at the river which was in spate after some recent snow. It's not like the sacred Narbada, I thought, but it is very beautiful even in winter. I missed seeing men in wet hitched-up loin cloths, and women in clinging soaked saris, bathing and washing clothes in the river. There were no dark-grey shambling water buffaloes, but I could see brown and white Herefordshire cattle lazily munching grass and looking every bit as indolent as water buffaloes. I was missing India, I had left a large part of my heart there. I was missing her villages, the acrid smell of burning cow dung, the round flat cow dung pats on the roofs of the houses drying in the sun to be used later as fuel. I was missing the village folk in their bullock carts, the noisy bazaars, the temples with lingams garlanded with marigolds. I was missing seeing the Indian women in coloured saris balancing water pots and bundles on their heads while walking upright and unhurried with smooth graceful elegant deportment, and the pan-chewing men in dhotis spitting out copious mouthfuls of vivid red saliva with unerring aim; and the lively laughing village children; and the babies with thick black charcoal circles smeared around their eyes to ward off the evil spirits. I was remembering the primitive Gonds who lived in the jungle where there were pepal, banyan, and teak trees, the crimson of the 'flame of the forest', with monkeys, parrots, blue jays and wild peacocks in the branches. Anyhow, I thought to myself, my new patients won't be speaking in a foreign tongue. I couldn't have been more wrong, the Forest of Dean dialect was to seem at first almost as foreign as Hindi. I left Huntsham Bridge and drove up the steep narrow winding road to Symonds Yat Rock, then on into the Forest of Dean to a new life, to new experiences, leaving India behind for ever, and I stayed in the Forest for nearly forty years. Of my early Forest of Dean days I have already written.*

Time, like an ever rolling stream, has not meandered since I was a boy, it has rushed along like the rapids below Symonds Yat, bringing changes as turbulent as the water in the rapids, and has borne away many of those men and women I knew before that day when I paused, and then crossed, Huntsham Bridge.

Chapter Twenty One

The Appointed Day

During the summer of 1948 we Forest of Dean doctors became head-hunters - all on account of the APPOINTED DAY.

July 5th 1948 was the appointed day, the day on which the National Health Service was inaugurated under the National Health Act of 1946, eight and a half years after I had settled down in the Forest of Dean. It was an overnight revolution. But then the Minister of Health, Aneurin Bevan, was a revolutionary, consumed with an intense deep passionate hatred and rebelliousness on account of the treatment miners had received over the years at the hands of greedy ruthless coal owners.

By the appointed day everybody in the country had been given a medical card on which was printed their NHS number (the same number which had been on their war-time identity card) and became entitled to free medical treatment - provided they had filled in their card and handed it to the doctor of their choice. It had been decided that general practitioners should be paid by a capitation fee - so much for every patient on their list, irrespective of whether they received any treatment or not. Hence there was a frantic rush by doctors to get as many patients, at so much a head, onto their list as soon as possible by the appointed day; so, for a few weeks we became head-hunters. There was also haste by many people to get onto a doctor's list. Aneurin Bevan had promised that everybody could have anything they wanted from the health service, and it would be FREE. Some were very anxious to cash in on that promise. Aneurin Bevan did not say that they were only entitled to what the doctors prescribed.

During the early months of the health service there was a rush by some people to doctors' surgeries asking for this and that, insisting they were entitled to them, and demanding their rights. There were acrimonious arguments between general practitioners and insistent patients. Many stories about it were floating around, possibly spread by people who disagreed with the implications of the National Health Service. There was the tale of the bald-headed sailors who were getting fitted with free wigs, which they subsequently flogged for cash in Port Said or somewhere. When they returned to their home port they demanded another wig. "But you had one only three months ago", the doctor would say. "It blew overboard during a gale", was the reply. Then there was the story, probably apocryphal, of the woman who was sitting in a doctor's crowded waiting room assiduously pulling her hair out by the roots, tugging out one hair at a time. She was watched by the other patients who were fascinated, wincing at each vicious tug. At length one man could contain himself no longer. "Why are you pulling your hair out?" he asked, "Well," the woman replied, "I've had dentures, spectacles, a hearing aid, an abdominal belt, surgical corsets, a walking aid and a truss. I'll get a wig if it kills me." Eventually things settled down and doctor-patient relationships became more amicable. It was a boon for doctors not to have the bother of sending out bills and to have no bad debts. To be able to order any necessary drugs, however expensive, to patients who would otherwise find it difficult to pay for them, was a relief, and a source of satisfaction to the doctor as well as to the patient. It was a considerable benefit to patients with chronic conditions on long term treatment. The situation before the appointed day was quite absurd. A man who was a wage earner could, under Lloyd George's National Insurance Act of 1911, get free health treatment, but not his wife or children. A lot of poor people benefitted after the appointed day. Mr and Mrs Charlie Fox, of the Rocks, Clearwell, were a delightful elderly couple, both of them very deaf. When I paid them my monthly visit I had to shout and yell at them before they could hear what I was saying. I thought hearing aids would be a boon for them, so I arranged for them both to be fitted with them. The first time I visited them after they had been supplied, they were both all smiles and very grateful, and I didn't need to shout. A month later when I called they were not wearing them. "Where are your hearing aids?" I bawled down Charlie's ear. He opened a drawer and pointed to them. "Why aren't you wearing them?" I shouted. "Oh, we only quarrel when we do", replied Charlie.

The commitments under the National Health Service Act meant that a single-handed practice would be difficult for me to maintain, particularly as I was given surgical sessions at the two Forest of Dean hospitals by the South West Regional Hospital Board. I therefore went into partnership with two other doctors and moved from Parkend to Coleford and then to Newland. The doctor who followed me at Parkend was a young man, dedicated, able and conscientious, very popular and much loved by his patients. Unfortunately he developed that dread complaint recurrent manic depression, which eventually led to his death under tragic circumstances. Fond as his two partners were of him, a manic depressive colleague created problems. It is especially sad that in those days lithium, which can control the symptoms to a considerable degree, had not then been discovered.

On the appointed day every hospital in the country, voluntary and municipal, came under the control of the Ministry of Health. The Dilke Memorial Hospital in the Forest of Dean had at that time a matron who was a Scot, and therefore canny. When the future date of the appointed day was announced she reasoned that if the Ministry of Health was going to acquire all the assets of the Voluntary hospitals it would also have to acquire their debts. She took this reasoning to the House Committee well before the appointed day together with a list of things needed by the hospital but for which there was then no adequate finance. She pointed out that all could be obtained and the bills left over for the Ministry to pick up after the appointed day. The members of the House Committee were enthusiastic and very co-operative. So a lot of equipment was ordered, bedside cubical curtains were installed, the slippery polished floors in the wards and corridors were sand-papered, and much more was done. It was many months after the appointed day before the Ministry officials got round to dealing with the bills, by which time the House Committee had long since been dissolved.

High hopes were entertained for the future of the National Health Service, and for some years it developed and was much admired and even envied by other countries (with the exception of America who derided it). Unfortunately politics have eroded it, both external party politics and politics within the health service itself.

Chapter Twenty Two

Tom, Dick and Harriet and Others

Tom developed an odd type of jaundice. There were other similar cases in the Forest of Dean, and the cause was a mystery. Then it transpired that Fasciola hepatica was the culprit. Fasciola hepatica was the posh name for a liver fluke, five millimetres long. It caused inflammation of the bile-ducts, blocking them, and so causing jaundice. But Fasciola hepatica is the liver fluke that causes liver-rot in sheep. There were plenty of sheep roaming around the Forest of Dean. But how had Tom and the other victims managed to get infected with a fluke that caused liver-rot in sheep? That was the mystery. It was known that the eggs of the fluke passed out in the sheep's droppings and were washed into streams after heavy rain where they infested water-snails. But Tom and the others hadn't been eating any snails. Then Dr A T Hunt, the Medical Officer of Health for the Forest of Dean, turned detective, and solved the mystery. He discovered that Tom and all the other victims had one thing in common, they had all been eating watercress which they had not bought in a shop but had been gathered from streams in the Forest. The water-snails had contaminated the water-cress in the streams, and that is how the little fluke with the posh name had caused Tom's jaundice. Dr Hunt was a very clever sleuth, a real Sherlock Holmes. So, be warned, if you want to eat water-cress, buy it in a shop where it has been safely grown by a horticulturist, don't be tempted to gather it from Forest streams.

Dick was getting on for forty years of age when he became my patient. That was nearly thirty years ago. Dick had not had an easy childhood, it had been cruelly overshadowed by that dreadful disease osteomyelitis. It had attacked his shin-bone, the infection spreading up the marrow cavity from his ankle up to and into his knee joint. Osteomylitis could be a killer disease in those pre-antibiotic days, and required drastic treatment to prevent death from septicaemia which was then all too common. In Dick's case drastic treatment had saved his life, but it had necessitated the guttering of his shin bone from ankle to knee. Bone was chiseled away to expose the entire length of the marrow cavity from his ankle to his knee, leaving a dreadful open wound, and his knee joint was opened for drainage of the infection. Slowly, over the months, new bone had gradually formed to fill the exposed cavity. But the infection never completely subsided, he was left with a chronically infected bone which continued to discharge pus through a sinus which persisted over the years. All his life he had had to spend time cleansing and dressing his leg, as well as to endure the inconvenience of a permanently rigid knee joint.

Dick owned a boot and shoe shop in Broadwell where he also did repairs. His customers came not only from Broadwell, but from a distance away. He had a severe disability, but like so many physically handicapped people, he also had considerable strength of character. One night an arsonist set fire to his shop which was gutted. It was a terrible shock for him when all that was left of his little business was a burnt out shell. The loss was made even more difficult for him to bear when it transpired that the arsonist was his mentally deranged brother. But Dick got over the shock. Pulling himself together he found other premises and bravely restarted his business. Dick used to raise a lot of money for the Dilke Memorial Hospital and was a committee member of the League of Hospital Friends. He had seen so much of hospitals during his childhood that they had a special place in his heart. Despite his disability, Dick was never sorry for himself, was always ready to do some act of kindness for others, and greeted everyone with a smile. He has now retired from his business.

Thank goodness the old fashioned guttering operation that was performed on Dick when he was a child is no longer necessary, antibiotics, which had not then been discovered, have revolutionised the treatment and eliminated the death rate. The only surgery which is now sometimes needed is a small drill hole in the bone to let out any pus that may have formed. If antibiotics had been available during Dick's childhood, what a different childhood he would have had, what games and activities he could have enjoyed, what suffering he would have been saved from, suffering which Dick has borne over the years with quiet uncomplaining courage.

I was standing at the entrance to the Dilke Memorial Hospital one morning talking to one of the sisters when a large saloon car bedecked with white ribbons containing a bride and bridegroom drew up, followed a few minutes later by another car, similarly beribboned, containing several gaily dressed bridesmaids. The bride in her white gown emerged from the first car with difficulty helped by a solicitous and worried bridegroom who sported a large white rose in his buttonhole. Clutching her bouquet the bride came slowly towards the hospital entrance stopping on the way as though doubled up with pain. The sister I was talking to left me in a hurry and quickly reappeared with a wheelchair in which she placed the distressed bride, rushing her straight into the maternity delivery room. There was just time to get her wedding gown off as the baby's head started to emerge. The delivery was soon over, and Harriet, the bride, was put to bed in the ward, her bouquet placed on the bedside locker where it remained during Harriet's stay in hospital. It transpired that Harriet had started in labour sometime before she had left her parents' house for church. During the service, as she said "I will", the waters had broken leaving a pool on the church floor, much to the consternation and indignation of the vicar. But Harriet had made it - just. "Oh", the sister said to me, "it's an Old Forest of Dean custom".

Terry, who lived in a cottage in Joyford, had a Mum who, unlike Harriet, tended to dilly dally. Terry was an eleven year old, with an impish face, a full share of devilment, plenty of self assurance, and was a bit of a ragamuffin. I met him one day in the town and could hardly believe my eyes. He was wearing a suit, had a clean collar round a clean neck, his hair was plastered down with brilliantine, and he had a carnation in his buttonhole. "You're all dressed up this morning Terry", I said to him. "I be goin' to a weddin'", he informed me. "Whose?" I asked. "Me Mum and Dad's", he replied. Is this another Forest of Dean custom, I wondered.

Henry, an odd job man, lived in Upper Redbrook transporting himself from job to job on a bicycle. He was fond of cider, a bottle of which always accompanied him on his bicycle rounds. Like so many people who live alone he liked nothing better than talking to anyone patient enough to listen. He it was who told me that Swan Pool, between Cherry Orchard and Upper Redbrook, was haunted. If you pass the pool at midnight, he said, you would hear the sound of a child crying and then see the figure of a woman with a child in her arms emerge slowly from the water draped in green slimy water-weed. Then a large black hound comes out of the woods near by, gallops around the pool then disappears into the woods again. Henry did not always live in Upper Redbrook, he had spent his childhood the other side of the Forest of Dean near Littledean at a place called Greenbottom. He told me that when he was a boy he and his pals used to wander about in the Forest nearby. They met gypsies there, and watched the charcoal burners that frequented the area. They played near St. Anthony's Well which is not a wishing well but has healing properties, with a reputation which went back many centuries. To drink the water was good for rheumatism, to bathe in it cured skin diseases. Henry, grinning, said that he and the other boys used to increase the potency of the healing powers of the water. "How did you manage to do that?" I asked him. "We used to pee in it", he replied.

Do trees and plants have emotions? Nearly twenty years ago Backster in America claimed that they do proving it to his satisfaction under scientific laboratory conditions. Many devoted gardeners talk to their plants and believe that the plants respond. C G Jung said that for him trees and plants were the thoughts of God, their beauty revealing to him the mind of the Creator. Perhaps trees and plants are not just trees and plants. There is a small clump of trees in a field adjacent to where I lived in Newland. One day some boys from the village were playing in the field and one of them started to climb one of the trees. When he was a good way up the tree the branch that was supporting him gave way. He fell and as his body hit the ground his neck broke. He died instantly. Everyone in the village was shocked at the tragedy which cast a gloom over the village, and the tree out of which he had fallen, started to wither and die. In a few months it was quite dead and bleak and bare, the other trees around it being perfectly healthy. Why did the tree die? Is it possible that it felt remorse or grief over what had happened, or was it just a coincidence? Did it die from grief? Who can tell? But it was a strange thing to have happened and I don't think it was just a coincidence.

John was a mongol. He was in his late twenties when I first knew him. His

mother had died when he was a small boy, his father caring for him afterwards. Simple hearted and friendly, he was more intelligent than most
people realised. Like many mongols he loved music. He was also religious,
and could follow the church service in the Prayer Book. His father's great
hobby, which John shared, was collecting butterflies and moths. John
could tell the names of the different kinds. Some summer nights he and his
father would go into the forest, spread out a white sheet and light a bright
primus lamp. This attracted moths who would settle on the white sheet.
John was happy and smiling, and loved the forest. Would it have been right
to have denied him all the joy he experienced if his mother had aborted
him in the early part of her pregnancy? Yet that is what some people these
days would have advocated.

Canon Wyndham Jones, Vicar of Christchurch, could be seen, some
years back, outside the village school at the junction where the five roads
meet, as the children came out of school. He stood in the middle of the
road, tall, elderly and distinguished looking, wearing a long cassock and
with a red beret on his head. He was acting as a self-appointed traffic war-
den, protecting the children as they crossed the road after coming out of
school before the days of the lolly-pop-man. I met him one day as he was
walking from Symonds Yat rock direction towards Christchurch. I stopped
the car and offered him a lift. He thanked me, and opening the door on the
passenger side he put one foot inside. Then he hesitated and said "Have
you ever driven me before?" "No, Vicar", I answered. Crossing himself he
muttered "In the name of the Father, the Son, and the Holy Ghost - just
to be on the safe side, doctor". During one Sunday Service he announced,
"Next Sunday is Harvest Thanksgiving Sunday. The good Lord will be
pleased to receive in the church the products of your labours in the shape
of fruit, vegetables and flowers. The good Lord would also be grateful for
a load of horse-manure, but He does not think it suitable for it to be placed
in his church. So if it could be put in the vicarage garden, I will deal with it
for Him". He was a much loved man, simple-hearted, delighting in
humour, and loving humanity. I had a call to a house in Christchurch one
morning. I knocked on the door which was opened by a young woman with
tears pouring down her cheeks. "I'm sorry to be so upset, doctor" she said,
"but I've just heard that Canon Wyndham Jones died in his sleep last
night."

My telephone rang one morning just before nine o'clock. A voice asked
"Is that the butcher?" to which I replied "have you got the wrong number
or are you being abusive?" There was a little pause, and then the voice
asked "Who am I talking to?" to which I replied "the doctor". There was
another pause and then I heard the voice say to itself "Ooh - bloody 'ell",
and then rang off.

Sister Ruane, who was at the Dilke Hospital some years ago, was a very
efficient sister, and knew it. She had a very well developed no-nonsense
authoritative air about her, which no patient felt like challenging. One
incident which she later told me of, occurred one Saturday afternoon and
did her ego a lot of good. A man dressed in an open shirt, shorts and san-

dals turned up at casualty. He was spending the weekend at the Speech House Hotel, a mile up the road. "I've got something in my eye, sister", he said, "it's under the upper lid. Would you please get it out for me? And please, don't send for a doctor." "Sit you down there" said Sister, brusquely, and hold your head right back." The man sat down as ordered and obediently held his head back. Sister everted the upper lid revealing a bit of grit which she removed with a wisp of damp cotton wool. "You can't go yet", she said firmly, "I'm going to wash out the eye with normal saline". This she proceeded to do. "You can't go yet", she said again, "I must enter your details in the register."

"Name?" this was supplied.

"Age", this was also supplied.

"Address", A London address was given.

"Occupation?" "Senior Ophthalmic Surgeon, Moorfields Eye Hospital" her patient replied. Collapse of Sister Ruane. As he got to the exit door he turned, smiled at her, and said "Thank you, Sister, you did it very nicely. And thank you again for not sending for a doctor. I don't trust doctors".

On Friday February 17th 1984 in the Church of the Good Shepherd at Broadwell, we said farewell to Arthur Baynham, an eighty year old Freeminer. The church was packed to overflowing with his Forest friends. I look back to over forty years of his friendship. I remember him first as the devoted son of his widowed mother, who was the licensee of the Rising Sun Inn at Broadwell. As a young man Arthur had worked in the Cannop colliery, but ill health forced him to leave the mine. When war broke out he was medically unfit for the forces, and served as a special constable instead. After the death of his mother, he took over the Rising Sun, looking after his invalid sister. When she died he left the Rising Sun and started a taxi service. Cars had an almost crazy fascination for Arthur, both for driving and tinkering about with them. Later he became a car driving instructor. Many are the kindnesses Arthur showed me over the years. To think of Arthur Baynham is to think of kindness. After the war the Americans, who had invaded the Forest, sold off very cheaply a lot of their equipment rather than take it back to America. Arthur bought a large army front-wheel-drive truck. He bought it for a song, was very proud of it. During that terrible winter of 1947, when for weeks the Forest was buried under many feet of snow, covering the hedges and the sign posts, isolating villages, and making the roads impassable, Arthur found his army truck very useful. One night I had an urgent call from the Dilke Hospital. Driving there by car was out of the question, so I rang up Arthur. He turned up in his army truck. With great difficulty he managed to get me to the hospital. He waited to take me back. As we started back he said that the roads around Speech House were so bad that he was going to try a short cut he knew through the forest. We left the road and drove down a path into the forest. It was hard going, and eventually the truck ran into a huge snow drift and stuck. We tried to dig it out with no success. My spade hit a hard object which I uncovered. It was a sign post which read "Poison Gas - Keep Out". During the war the Americans had stored thousands of tons of poison gas in the forest. When they left they left the gas behind. Fortunately it never became necessary to use it. It took several years to clear it all away. I was told that it was dumped in the North Sea, where it probably still is. However, to return to Arthur's truck, we had to abandon it in the drift and trudge back in our wellies, hard going in that deep snow. It was very eerie in the forest, there was a stillness and an enveloping silence; everywhere one looked there was a ghostly whiteness lit up by the moonlight, the snow clad trees looked gaunt and sombre and menacing. We saw the bodies of birds which had died of cold and hunger, and a few dead sheep. The truck was retrieved later, after the thaw. That is one memory I have of Arthur. All memories of him are of his kindness. He was everybody's friend, especially to those in trouble. Quietly, patiently, with a smile he went about helping people. In these restless, turbulent, greedy days, it is good to remember with affection the genuineness and humbleheartedness of Arthur Baynham, the good Samaritan of the Forest.

Chapter Twenty Three

Fraser and Jack

This book has been about people. Are dachsunds people? I don't know. But they have personality and the Oxford dictionary defines personality as "being a person". So I suppose dachsunds are persons. Fraser and Jack were dachsunds.

Fraser was my constant companion for twelve years from his puppyhood, I saw him being born. When he died I missed him so much I vowed I would never have a dog again. But somebody wiser than me just dumped Jack on me. He and I became inseperable for twelve and a half years. Thus for a quarter of a century I always had a dachsund as a shadow, following me everywhere. If I got up to leave a room, I would be followed, if I went to spend a penny, a dachsund would be waiting patiently outside the toilet. They came everywhere in the car with me, and if left in the car, would guard it fiercely. They sat quietly under my desk in my consulting room while I was seeing patients, they followed me round the wards in the hospital, and sat with me while I was seeing Outpatients. Sometimes a nervous rather scared child, overwhelmed by nurses' uniforms and doctors' white coats, would be brought unwillingly and with some resistance to Outpatients. I had only to call Fraser or Jack from under the desk to shake hands with the child, to allow him to be stroked, when fear and apprehension would disappear because children love animals, especially they like touching them. Fraser and Jack were fond of children. Jack did not only shake hands, but he sat up on his haunches while his head and back were being gently stroked. You may wonder why there was no objection from the Matron about a dog following me around in hospital. The answer is quite simple, she had two dachsunds herself, one of them, Pauline, being Fraser's mother, and they followed her around and sat with her in her office. The Daks were very popular with the patients. One patient, a Miss I Riches, was so impressed by Fraser, that she wrote a paragraph about him for a woman's magazine, for which she received a guinea. She sent me a cutting which I still have, it reads:

"When I was in hospital recently, the monotony was frequently relieved by the antics of the surgeon's dog, Fraser. He would not be left outside the ward door and would bark until someone let him in. One day I tried to make friends with him, but his master told me he was only friendly when he had been introduced, which Fraser immediately proved by placing his paw in my hand. Then his master said, "Fraser has only ever bitten one man - a police inspector - all the constables clubbed together to buy him a medal". He swears that the dog still wears it!"

It is true that Fraser bit a police inspector, but what she wrote about the medal is fictitious. He certainly wore a medallion which indicated his membership of the Tailwaggers Club. The police inspector was a dour, humourless and rather surly man, not very popular with anybody. He came to see me one day with a laceration on the back of his hand. "Your dog did that", he said rather aggresively. "How come?" I asked. "Well," he said, "I just opened the door of your car and when I put my hand inside the dog bit me". He could give me no adequate reason why he had wanted to poke about inside my car. I told him that the dog was guarding my property and it was therefore a perfectly legal bite. The only other person to whom both Fraser and Jack took marked objection was any clergyman wearing a cassock. They didn't bite but just barked vigorously around their ankles. I can't understand why clergymen like to go about looking like Dracula, except that they do seem to enjoy dressing up. They always wear black cassocks, why can't they choose a more cheerful colour? Anyhow, both Fraser and Jack disapproved of black cassocks. It was the black cassocks they objected to, not the person inside. Whether they would have objected to a different colour, such as pale pink, lavender, or tory-blue, I just don't know.

Although our milkman delivered milk it was whisky that he drank himself, quite a lot of it, being sometimes far from sober on his morning round. One day he developed D.T.'s and was admitted to a room in the Dilke Memorial Hospital. He was very hallucinated, seeing animals of all sorts and sizes and shapes around him. Next day when I went to visit him, the sister told me he was much quieter and seemed a lot better. I went into the side ward to have a look at him, followed of course by Fraser. The patient looked at me, then he turned his eyes on Fraser, immediately gave a yell, pointed to Fraser with a trembling finger, and started hallucinating again.

Jack and I used to go for long walks over the fields around Newland. He was a good rabbiter, would catch a rabbit, then triumphantly and gallantly walk back home with it in his mouth, his head held high and his tail very erect. When he tarried behind me on a walk, investigating some very attractive smell, I would whistle to him to come along. He knew my whistle and would immediately obey. Alongside one of the fields was a small copse wherein lived a jackdaw who would copy my whistly exactly. Jack was often very bemused when while walking beside me he also heard me whistling from the copse.

When Fraser was about ten years old he developed a displaced disc in his back, his hind legs became paralysed so that I had to carry him about in a basket for about three months. One day a visitor called bringing a lady poodle with her. Fraser looked at the lady poodle from his basket and his tail gave a feeble wag, the first sign of any movement of the back half of his body for three months. After that he steadily improved and was able to get about but not to cock a hind leg, having to squat like a bitch, which he found very humiliating. When Jack was about ten years old he started to drag his hind legs one day and was obviously in much pain. I realised that he too was developing a displaced disc like Fraser had done so I immediately called the vet, who gave him an injection of cortisone. Next morning Jack's pain had gone, his legs were normal and he did not look back. How I wished that cortisone had been available for Fraser twelve years before, it would have saved him much suffering.

Dachsunds may not be people but they certainly are persons, of that there is no shadow of doubt, the Oxford dictionary proving it. I expect it applies to other breeds also and to those dogs of no known breed.

ENVOI

Time like an ever rolling stream
Bears all its sons away.

H.F. Lyte

What a motley collection of individuals I have been telling you about, each one so different from any other in personality, character and background. Time like an ever rolling stream has now swept them all away, as it eventually sweeps away all the many millions around the world; each one of them, also, different from each other, each one unique. Existence seems to be a tension between opposites, and humanity to be Janus-faced. One face of Man is its bright benevolent face, with the spirit of man reaching upwards, searching for truth and for freedom of mind, for freedom from materialism, tyranny and totalitarianism, using science to make life pleasanter, healthier, easier and more tolerable. Spread out through all the world are simple hearted humble hidden souls whose hearts are true and good, full of neighbourliness, love and compassion. The opposite face of man is the dark malevolent face, making science dangerous and threatening, revealing itself in bloody wars, in violence, in massacres and mob frenzy, in terrorism, in unimaginative cruelty, in ruthless greed, corruption, lust for power, in the evil inside the vicious psychopath, the sadist, the pervert. Everything has its opposite: goodness and evil, love and hatred, forgiveness and revenge, peace and war, beauty and ugliness, happiness and misery, male and female, day and night, birth and death. Why this should be so is a mystery. Another mystery is Time, the ever rolling stream. What is Time? What was there before there was Time? That Time never had a beginning is incomprehensible and irrational, a metaphysical problem. Only the materialists, the rationalists, the dogmatists, the bigots, the fundamentalists pretend to know all the answers. But they cannot explain time, or eternity or infinity, or why mankind has two opposite faces. There is no answer, it is all wrapped up in numinous mystery. Everything has its opposite, except, maybe, TIME.

Ask not the clock
What is the meaning
Of its "tick-tock".
Content be you, as I, to mark the sliding
Of Time. No chime
Breaks Life, now gliding
Quietly through our dream "forget-me-nots".
Ask meaning
Only of Life, the river which flows forever,
Bearing away into Eternity   **F.W. Harvey**
Soul-Boats!   *The Forest of Dean Poet.*